T0209531

62

DAYS IN THE WORD

Richard A. Lynn

WESTBOW
PRESS®
A DIVISION OF THOMAS NELSON
& ZONDERVAN

WestBow Press books may be ordered through booksellers or by contacting:

WestBow Press
A Division of Thomas Nelson & Zondervan
1663 Liberty Drive
Bloomington, IN 47403
www.westbowpress.com
844-714-3454

ISBN: 978-1-6642-6122-8 (sc)
ISBN: 978-1-6642-6123-5 (hc)
ISBN: 978-1-6642-6121-1 (e)

Library of Congress Control Number: 2022905076

Print information available on the last page.

WestBow Press rev. date: 03/30/2022

DEDICATION

I would like to dedicate this book to my grandson Sebastian. I want him to always have some words of mine that he can turn to, even when I am no longer around. I love you buddy!

ACKNOWLEDGMENTS

I first and foremost want to say thanks to God for choosing me to be a vessel for His word. Without Him, this couldn't happen. I would also like to thank my wonderful wife, Andrea, who helped me every step of the way. Also thanks to my three daughters. They helped me more than they even know. Thanks to everyone at the Buchanan County Jail. They supported me and encouraged me to do this. I can't forget to say thanks to my Hope Wesleyan church family. They are a big part of my walk with the Lord. Lastly, thanks to Westbow for all the hard work they did. They helped bring this vision to life. They are wonderful and I am glad to be working with them. Thank you!

THE INTRODUCTION

I am taking a step of faith by putting this little devotional together. I am not some brilliant writer or even a person with several degrees. I am just a man who's saying yes to the leading of the Holy Spirit. I am going to be real with you too. I have worked in a jail since July 2001. I have seen broken people and their many wasted years. I also know that I was one decision away from being in that way of life too. I struggled growing up as a teenager, and I also had my battle with substance abuse. I haven't touched a drop of alcohol since May 2007, so I know I can relate a little bit to both sides. I know the struggle, and now I know about getting set free. I am going to give you some scriptures and some devotional thoughts. I hope they help point you to Jesus and what He has already done for you. God has made a way for you to live a better life—a life more abundant and with purpose. I try to explain the scriptures in a practical way so you can see your life through the lens of the Holy Spirit too. You can also look up the scriptures provided in other translations so you can compare them. You will figure out the ones that God gives you the most clarity with. His Word is life changing.

I believe there's no reason why an inmate can't leave jail different from when he or she came in. It's going to take a connection with God for that to happen. I can help point you in the right direction, but it's up to you to say yes to Him. You can wash the mud off a pig but as soon as you let the pig go, it will head right back to the mud. That's its nature. That's who a pig is. The only way the same thing won't happen to you is for you to get a new nature. Only God can do that for you. My prayer is that this devotional will encourage you in the Lord and inspire you to become born again and receive your new nature from God. You won't even want to go back to the mud after that. Accepting Jesus into your heart is the only way to get started on the journey to your new way of life. You still have a pulse and breath in your lungs. That means there's still hope. Read through this devotional and pray often about that day. Use the next sixty-two days to get aligned with God. Take it one day at a time. The Holy Spirit of Acts is still the same. Be different in Jesus's Name!

> So be strong and courageous, all you who put your
> hope in the Lord! (Psalms 31:24 NLT)

DAY 1

When he had finished speaking, he said to Simon, "Now go out where it is deeper, and let down your nets to catch some fish." "Master," Simon replied, "we worked hard all last night and didn't catch a thing. But if you say so, I'll let the nets down again." And this time their nets were so full of fish they began to tear! (Luke 5:4–6 NLT)

When God gets into your boat (life), everything can change for you. However, you must be obedient to what He says. What He says might seem like it is impossible. It might seem crazy in your eyes. You have probably been striving your entire life so far and still haven't produced the kind of life you long for. Then God gets into your boat (life) and tells you to go deeper—to where you couldn't even touch the bottom if you fell in—and it's frightening to be out so far away from the shore.

Simon didn't have much faith in that idea, but he obeyed. You might have doubts. You might be afraid. You just need to obey anyway and let your net down where it is deep. You want to stay sober and out of jail? Then you will have to go where it is deeper—whatever that looks like for you. Maybe it's a move to a new town. Maybe it's going to church regularly, even if no one else will go with you. Maybe it's going back to school. Maybe these are all things you have tried before, but you tried them on your own. Or you might have been in the wrong waters (places). Pray about this. Get a vision from God in your heart. Then drop your net where it is deeper. Your action will bless you, and everyone around you will be blessed too. The blessing will overflow to others.

DAY 2

We can make our plans, but the Lord determines our steps. (Proverbs 16:9 NLT)

We can come up with good plans for our lives, but it will be the Lord who will determine the steps to get there. An example could be that you want to overcome addiction and stay sober forever. That's a very good plan to have for yourself, and it's God's will for you. For that to be successful, the Lord will have to determine your steps. He knows exactly what steps you will need to take for that to happen. That road might seem long. That road might get a little rough at times. That road might go through some dark tunnels. But that road will also be the most scenic and most beautiful road you will ever be on. Each step will make you better. Each step will transform you from the old way to the new way. We always want it all to happen right now, but He wants to take us on that road. On the road is where we will truly get to know the Father better. You want to be different? Then you will have to allow Him to show you how. Old keys can't unlock new doors.

Take hold of my instructions; don't let them go. Guard them, for they are the key to life. (Proverbs 4:13 NLT)

DAY 3

When you go out to fight your enemies and you face horses and chariots and an army greater than your own, do not be afraid. The Lord your God, who brought you out of the land of Egypt, is with you! When you prepare for battle, the priest must come forward to speak to the troops. He will say to them, "Listen to me, all you men of Israel! Do not be afraid as you go out to fight your enemies today! Do not lose heart or panic or tremble before them. For the Lord your God is going with you! He will fight for you against your enemies, and he will give you victory!" (Deuteronomy 20:1–4 NLT)

You are going to have a war on your hands. Your enemy is going to come at you. It won't be with chariots and horses; it will be in the form of substances that had you addicted and people who lead you astray. The battles of the war will be won or lost in the spiritual realm. That is where a lot of people mess up. They try to fight everything physically. That often leads to exhaustion, frustration, and depression. People will give up and give in. The key is to fight spiritually too. Your strength comes from God. God has already pulled you out of Egypt (the world you used to live in), and now He is equipping you for the battles you will face. The above passage contains a war cry for you to plant in your heart. Pray it daily, speak it often, and trust that God is fighting this with you. You have the victory. Jesus gave you that. Now you just have to keep it. It is easier to fight from the place of spiritual victory than it is to fight for victory in the natural.

Your war cry is this: Don't be scared. Don't be afraid. Don't panic or be terrified. The Lord, your God, is going with you. He'll fight for you. He'll help you win the battle over your enemies.

Now prepare yourself by connecting with God daily, through His word and in prayer. Trust Him.

You can also read through Psalm 31 for some extra encouragement.

> A final word: Be strong in the Lord and in his mighty power. (Ephesians 6:10 NLT)

DAY 4

Take control of what I say, O Lord, and guard my lips. (Psalms 141:3 NLT)

Zechariah said to the angel, "How can I be sure this will happen? I'm an old man now, and my wife is also well along in years." Then the angel said, "I am Gabriel! I stand in the very presence of God. It was he who sent me to bring you this good news! But now, since you didn't believe what I said, you will be silent and unable to speak until the child is born. For my words will certainly be fulfilled at the proper time." (Luke 1:18–20 NLT)

If you are always complaining or speaking negatively about everything, then ask God to set a guard over your mouth. It would be better to be quiet than to speak against yourself. Words are very powerful. God formed the worlds by His words and created us to talk for a reason. If you are currently dealing with some difficulties, then start by asking God to take control over your mouth each day. Then, after you have meditated on a scripture about your current situation, start speaking those words by faith rather than words of defeat. Then end each day praising Him and thanking Him for the victory. Speak life over yourself. Don't speak words of discontentment or doubt. The tongue is a lot more powerful than we think.

The tongue can bring death or life; those who love to talk will reap the consequences. (Proverbs 18:21 NLT)

DAY 5

Don't be afraid, for I am with you. Don't be
discouraged, for I am your God. I will strengthen
you and help you. I will hold you up with my
victorious right hand. (Isaiah 41:10 NLT)

When fear grips you, it can feel like you are losing control of
everything, that there's nothing you can do. When you are going
through anxious times like that, you can stand firmly on this
scripture. Start to declare this over yourself when that type of fear
tries to overcome you. Keep that heart of yours guarded by declaring
His Word instead of listening to the lies of the enemy. You and God
will get through this together. It's not always easy, but it's simple.
Trust Him with your life. He's got you with a victorious right hand.

DAY 6

You intended to harm me, but God intended it all
for good. He brought me to this position so I could
save the lives of many people. (Genesis 50:20 NLT)

I am not the perfect person to be writing anything about the Word
of God. I don't have a biblical studies degree, and I haven't pastored
a local church. I am just a child of God who has struggled with many
of the things I write about. I am learning how to overcome through
the teaching and equipping of the Holy Spirit. It is through Christ
that I can learn, overcome, and share with others. As I continue
my journey through life, I still have a lot of obstacles come against
me from time to time. Anxiety, fear, and depression still try to
contaminate my heart daily. The more I wrestle and struggle with
all of that, the stronger I become.

It's amazing how God will use the very thing that the enemy
uses to hurt a person to strengthen that person. My hope is that I
can encourage someone to keep the faith while walking along his
or her journey too. Maybe I can inspire someone to keep the faith
regardless of the situation, like Joseph did when he was thrown into
the pit before he became governor in the palace. In life, sometimes
pits happen. We all face the pits of life. I don't know anyone who is
immune to that, but God is present, even when pits happen. Keep
the faith, my friends. God is always good.

DAY 7

But blessed are those who trust in the Lord and have made the Lord their hope and confidence. They are like trees planted along a riverbank, with roots that reach deep into the water. Such trees are not bothered by the heat or worried by long months of drought. Their leaves stay green, and they never stop producing fruit. (Jeremiah 17:7–8 NLT)

If you haven't noticed lately, the world can be a very chaotic place to live in. Everyone is divided on every issue possible. The mental state of most Americans is starting to suffer, especially with all this COVID stuff going on. Anxiety is at an all-time high. Suicide attempts seem to be a daily thing these days. Substance abuse seems to be the answer a lot more people are choosing. Maybe you are even dealing with the news of a loved one's passing. The world around you can certainly seem rocky. Blessed are those who trust in the Lord regardless. Those people are deep in the water (Holy Spirit), and the heat of the world won't burn them. You can be rooted deep in the Holy Spirit and produce good fruit for everyone else around you. The Holy Spirit is vital to living the life God has called you to live. You can be blessed in the middle of the mess.

DAY 8

Our ancestors in Egypt were not impressed by the Lord's miraculous deeds. They soon forgot his many acts of kindness to them. Instead, they rebelled against him at the Red Sea. Even so, he saved them—to defend the honor of his name and to demonstrate his mighty power. (Psalms 106:7–8 NLT)

Whenever we find ourselves in a difficult situation, usually because of our own stupid decisions, we seem to forget everything God has done. We continue our rebellious ways. Maybe you ended up in a jail cell for one of those stupid decisions in the past. You connected with God while you were in there, but shortly after being released, the rebellion continued. Then you found yourself in that jail again.

The key words you need to focus on in the above scripture are "even so." The Israelites forgot about everything God had previously done and continued with their rebellious ways. *Even so*, God saved them from the Egyptian army. You are at a Red Sea moment in your life right now. The Red Sea represents an obstacle that is blocking your way to a new life, and the Egyptian army represents your past life. The situation looks hopeless. You can't see how God would make the way for you.

You are still in jail and frustrated with everything. Then all those past decisions are racing back upon you, creating anxiety, depression, and some sleepless nights. No matter what your past decisions were, no matter how you ended up back in jail, and no matter how you previously rebelled against God's ways, you have a loving Heavenly Father saying to you today, "Even so"! He didn't bring you to the Red Sea to destroy your life and make it harder on you. He did it so you can pass through the waters, and then He can drown everything in the past that is chasing you. He will part the Red Sea for you. He will drown that past and give you a new start to life. You don't deserve His grace, but even so He will demonstrate His power in your life for His name's sake. He will bless you and use you to help others turn to Him.

Faith moves you forward. Quit turning back to those Egyptian ways that keep you in bondage. You are loved very much by God—even more than you realize. This is your Red Sea moment. Make the decision to finally keep moving forward despite what it looks like in the natural and trust that He is your way maker. Don't go back to Egypt ever again. Let God use the water to cleanse you from that past way of life. Be baptized into a new way of life— "even so."

> But if we confess our sins to him, he is faithful and just to forgive us our sins and to cleanse us from all wickedness. (1 John 1:9 NLT)

DAY 9

For this is how God loved the world: He gave his one and only Son, so that everyone who believes in him will not perish but have eternal life. (John 3:16 NLT)

If you have a glass of cold water and pour hot water into it, the temperature of that cold water changes. If you have a glass of hot water and pour cold water into it, the temperature of that water also changes. I believe that we have that ability too. If you walk into a hostile work environment, pour some of God's goodness into the place. The environment will change. If you walk into a place where everyone seems depressed, pour some of God's goodness into the place; that environment will also change. When I didn't deserve it, God poured His love into me. That changed me forever.

That same spirit is with you wherever you go. Pour it all over the place. You may do this by listening. You might pray with someone. You might change the subject of a conversation. You might make a joke. You might quote a scripture passage that someone desperately needs to hear. Complaining, gossiping, and arguing over stupid stuff will not glorify God. Be a kingdom builder. Remember God poured His love out for you. The way we can thank Him is by pouring into others what God has poured into us. Love is the most powerful force on earth. Don't just make room for God in your life, but rather give Him the room. You are a difference maker.

DAY 10

–◆–◆–◆–◆–◆–◆–◆–

Seeing their faith, Jesus said to the paralyzed man,
"My child, your sins are forgiven." (Mark 2:5 NLT)

The guy was paralyzed, and that is exactly how we all are when we lose our identity. The devil doesn't want you to know who you really are. He wants you to be defined by what the world says you should be. That could lead to a whole host of problems. A good example of this could be professional athletes. They quit playing their sports and they often lose their identities. Then they start to search for ways to fill that gap in their lives and they become paralyzed or enslaved to the ways of the world. They turn to other things, such as drugs, sex, alcohol, gambling, or any other type of pleasure-seeking activity to try to fill the gap in their hearts that only Jesus can fill.

Everyone needs that type of void filled in their hearts by connecting with God. Nothing else can ever do that. Nothing can replace that love. Who you really are inside makes a big difference on how you live. The devil can't push you around anymore. You are not what you do or did. You are who God says you are. Any gossip about you won't matter anymore. What others think of you doesn't matter as much. You can't really get offended either. You won't need anything else to give you joy or pleasure either. All of that will come from your Heavenly Father. Only what He says about you is what truly matters. Once Jesus told the guy who he really was and that he was forgiven, it set him free. You don't need anything but a relationship with God to get through this world. Yes, we do need others who are willing to lift us up when we are down and care enough to rip a roof off the place to get us to Jesus. We all need those people because sometimes we do lose our way. I am here to help rip that roof off and get you at the feet of Jesus so you can be set free too. You are forgiven. You are loved. You are chosen. You are fearfully and wonderfully made. You are healed. You are free from the bondage of sin. You are a child of God!

DAY 11

You prepare a table before me in the presence of my enemies; You anoint my head with oil; My cup runs over. Surely goodness and mercy shall follow me All the days of my life; And I will dwell in the house of the Lord Forever. (Psalms 23:5–6 NKJV)

God has prepared a table for you, even amid everything that the enemy has surrounded you with. You can pull up a chair and sit at His table. You can eat what He must feed you. You can consume His goodness and the bread of life (His Word). The only way the enemy can sit at this table is if you invite him to. The world can be falling apart, and you can still be sitting in His presence, remaining peaceful and strong regardless of world events. People can talk badly about you and the only way it truly can impact your life is if you let it into your heart. You focus more on what they say than on what He said, that's an invitation to your table. The news spread fear and worry about COVID-19. You invite the enemies of fear and worry to your table by meditating on what they spewed out instead of what God has already said in His Word. You get a bad report from the doctor. You believe that report over God's. Then you have sickness eating with you. You pray for blessings, but your own mouth speaks doubts. You have contaminated faith at the table. You aren't feeling the best, so you take some type of substance to lift you up. You have addiction and all his friends sitting next to you.

All of this can block you from His presence. God didn't leave the table, but you invited the crowd to get in the way. God wants to anoint you and appoint you for great things. That's what's taking place at the table. The oil is the baptizing of the Holy Spirit upon you. Your cup will overflow with blessings so everyone else around you can be impacted and see God in a tangible way. Sitting at His table will change you and everyone that you pour into. Jesus drank the cup of bitterness that the enemy brought to the table so we could drink from the cup of blessings that He brought to the table.

> Saying, "Father, if it is Your will, take this cup away from Me; nevertheless, not My will, but Yours, be done." (Luke 22:42 NKJV)

He died so that we could live in the house of the God forever. Forever means right now too. Look behind you and you will see two people who God brought to the table to sit with you. They are goodness and mercy. Don't give the enemy an invitation to the table God has prepared for you. Nothing good ever happens when the enemy is invited into your life.

DAY 12

After the death of Moses, the Lord's servant, the Lord spoke to Joshua son of Nun, Moses' assistant. He said, "Moses my servant is dead. Therefore, the time has come for you to lead these people, the Israelites, across the Jordan River into the land I am giving them. I promise you what I promised Moses: 'Wherever you set foot, you will be on land I have given you—'" (Joshua 1:1–3 NLT)

Moses has now passed away, so Joshua gets the assignment of leading the Israelites into the Promised Land. They need to cross the Jordan in order to do that. Imagine the possible thoughts that started going through Joshua's head. His friend and mentor is no longer there with him. The one everyone thought would be leading all the Israelites into the Promised Land is no longer available. It wasn't just the fact they had to physically cross the Jordan. That wasn't going to be the biggest problem for Joshua. Joshua's challenge would be to move their hearts and souls from one way of life to other. The land is great, but there will be giants to face. God has chosen Joshua to lead them. He had a great mentor. He was called and chosen. He knows the word better than a lot of the other people. He knows what it is like to be in bondage to the enemy. He had to lead others away from that way of life.

Let's put this in a practical way. How would you lead your family across the Jordan? How will you lead the people you meet in your life who are struggling? How will you lead in your workplace? What about within your local church or in your community? Everyone God puts you in front of will have a different mindset. Some will be younger. Some will be older. Some will be close to God, and some won't know anything about Him. You will need to be able to lead them from where they are and from where you are in your spiritual walk. Fear will be the biggest giant you will encounter, and everyone you lead will eventually have to face that giant too. The Jordan isn't very deep, wide, or long, but you could still drown in it very easily. You must not be afraid to be the one in your family to take that first step to the life God has prepared for you. God will provide the way. Once you cross into the new way of life, be ready to face those giants of life: fear, addiction, anxiety, depression, and everything bad the enemy can send against you.

God is raising up a remnant of Joshua. He will be going to the streets and highways to find them too. If the church will bow to fear and close the doors, where will He find them? He will find them in the streets and in the jails. You can be a Joshua, no matter what you have done or been through. This is a word from God to you today.

> "Study this Book of Instruction continually. Meditate on it day and night so you will be sure to obey everything written in it. Only then will you prosper and succeed in all you do. This is my command—be strong and courageous! Do not be afraid or discouraged. For the Lord your God is with you wherever you go." (Joshua 1:8–9 NLT)

DAY 13

"Look, the Ark of the Covenant, which belongs to the Lord of the whole earth, will lead you across the Jordan River! Now choose twelve men from the tribes of Israel, one from each tribe. The priests will carry the Ark of the Lord, the Lord of all the earth. As soon as their feet touch the water, the flow of water will be cut off upstream, and the river will stand up like a wall." (Joshua 3:11–13 NLT)

When you are about to enter your new way of life, it can look like it is going to be a big-time struggle. The Israelites were about to cross the Jordan and enter the Promised Land. They needed to trust that God would clear the way through once again. They just saw Him do it at the Red Sea, but they needed to have faith that He would do it again. They needed to know that He didn't just make the way for them before but that He is the way maker. That's who He is and not what He does from time to time.

You don't even need twelve priests to carry the Ark ahead of you. Stir up the spirit of God within you and trust the prompts on the inside. Lift His great name, which is the name of Jesus, then step into the waters ahead of you. The waters holding you back will stop, and you will walk across on dry ground. You must be willing to step in the water first.

Faith is assurance that God will do what He says. If He says that you are heading into a new way of life, then that's exactly what will happen. You need to take a step of faith forward into the river of the unknown. Get a word in your heart, lift up a praise, and go for it! Step into what a lot of other people would sink in. He is the way maker!

DAY 14

God is our refuge and strength, always ready to help in times of trouble. So, we will not fear when earthquakes come and the mountains crumble into the sea. Let the oceans roar and foam. Let the mountains tremble as the waters surge! (Psalms 46:1–3 NLT)

He is always present and ready to help in times of trouble. It doesn't matter what is going on in the world around you because the presence of God will be right there with you. Do not let fear of the situation distract you from that truth. Everything might seem like it's falling apart, but you won't be shaken. Stand on the truth of God's promises: that He loves you and that He is always present. Declare that in times of trouble. You are going to make it through this highly anxious time. You don't need to fear the worst because God has already given you the best.

> For this is how God loved the world: He gave his one and only Son, so that everyone who believes in him will not perish but have eternal life. (John 3:16 NLT)

You can put your name in this verse instead of the word *world*. Even if you were the only one He could save from sin and bring healing to, Jesus would have still gone to the cross. You are worth everything to Him.

DAY 15

I will guide you and teach you the way you should
go. I will give you good advice and watch over you
with love. (Psalm 32:8 NIRV)

We all want God's divine direction in our lives. That type of life is
exactly how we should all be living. How can you develop that kind
of connection with your Heavenly Father? It's by spending time with
Him throughout the day and by studying His instruction manual.
I have often struggled with this in my walk with God. Uncertainty,
doubts, fear and distraction have all influenced my decisions. That
leaves me confused and frustrated about the direction my life should
be going. I have found that usually you will know as you go. You
start doing small things by faith and next thing you know you are at
a new place in your life. You do need to get a vision and a purpose in
your heart from God. That's the end, but how you get there consists
of a series of steps that God ordains, in addition to getting back on
track from all the wrong turns you make along the way. Let the
Lord direct you into His love and presence every day. Next thing
you know, you will be at the right place at the right time. You will
just know this is the right way.

Whenever I got inside my head instead of my heart, that's when I
messed up. When I first started getting close to God, everything just
happened. I started reading and attending a church. Then one day I
started going to my current church. My daughter went there with a
friend a few times, so I went to check it out. I have been there ever
since, and I didn't even plan on that happening. This is God's divine
direction. I wanted to get a part-time job, so I prayed about it. The
answer was to serve in the community, so I looked online. I found
a need for Meals on Wheels delivery drivers, and it worked with my

schedule. God's divine direction. I was on a run one day and saw an older lady out walking. I felt a prompt to go pray with her. I didn't know her, and I have never seen her again. I told her that I felt led to pray for her and asked if there was something I could pray with her about. She said her sister has cancer, so we prayed on the side of the street for her sister. I don't know what happened after that, but I did that by faith. There's a lot more I could share, but you get the idea.

This is one of many examples of times when I missed it and I knew it. I was meeting with the pastor on a weekly basis. I was going to study to go into the ministry full time. Everything was set up and ready to go. I let my head get in the way of the faith in my heart. I decided not to pursue it any longer. How do I know I missed it? It hasn't ever left my heart, and I can't stop thinking about it. Maybe I will get back on track with that soon, but I am wrestling with my flesh on it. Is it God's plan or my plan? The conviction of the Holy Spirit— God's divine direction—is how I know. Having that discernment is important to live the life God is calling you to. Just start by spending time in prayer and in His word. You will be overwhelmed with His love and develop a patience for His plan. His ways are always the best ways.

> My thoughts are not like your thoughts. And your ways are not like my ways, announces the Lord. The heavens are higher than the earth. And my ways are higher than your ways. My thoughts are higher than your thoughts. (Isaiah 55:8–9 NIRV)

DAY 16

❖◆❖◆❖

> He came into the very world he created, but the world didn't recognize him. He came to his own people, and even they rejected him. But to all who believed him and accepted him, he gave the right to become children of God. They are reborn—not with a physical birth resulting from human passion or plan, but a birth that comes from God. (John 1:10–13 NLT)

You might be so focused on getting out of your current circumstances that you can't even recognize that God is trying to get in. God doesn't show up in your life exactly like you expect Him to. He came into the world in the ordinary way. He came as a baby and lived as man. He set aside His divinity to show how to live by the power of the Holy Spirit. That's not exactly how everyone expected the Savior to come. Most people missed it and rejected Him. They were looking to be saved from the Romans physically, but God needed to set them free spiritually.

Maybe you are an inmate currently in jail. You keep looking for a way to get out physically, but God might be trying to get in spiritually while you are in there. No, the conditions aren't good, but the condition of your spirit is much more important. If you were released physically but remained in jail spiritually, locked up by the enemy and unable to really live, that would just lead to more trouble and, worse yet, eternal separation from God. Why should jail be any different than church? A person should leave church different from when he or she arrived. A seed of faith should be planted somehow, and the physical separation from family is just a minor example of being separated from God.

Most of you aren't physically in jail, but you are spiritually in jail. You could be in a prison of your past that won't let you move on. You could be in the shackles of addiction. You could have financial debt that you are killing yourself trying to get out of. All of these are examples of things that would be great to get out of, but they won't matter if you are eternally separated from God. Take a moment today and look for all the ways that God is showing up in your life. Journal them and then record your thoughts. Then make the decision to surrender your heart to Him. Time is always ticking, so don't wait any longer. You read this to the end. That's your first example of God showing up in your life today.

> Turn my eyes from worthless things and give me life through your word. (Psalms 119:37 NLT)

DAY 17

> "You shall not take the name of the Lord your God
> in vain, for the Lord will not hold him guiltless who
> takes His name in vain." (Exodus 20:7 NKJV)

This means a lot more than just using His name as a swear word. It is about how you live your life after you have accepted Jesus Christ into your heart as your Lord and Savior. You asked Jesus into your heart. You have been baptized in the name of Jesus. You ask God to fill you with the Holy Spirit. Then you proceed to live your life in the opposite way. You fight with your neighbor. Who's your neighbor? Anyone God puts in your life. Maybe you still talk badly about people as if you're the perfect one. There's only one perfect one and that is Jesus. We are called to be witnesses and not judges. How can a person wear a cross on his or her necklace but crucify others with his or her actions? You can't say you are living in the name of Jesus and steal, kill, and destroy others. That's not God's way.

> "The thief's purpose is to steal and kill and destroy.
> My purpose is to give them a rich and satisfying
> life." (John 10:10 NLT)

Stealing physically is bad enough, but you can also steal someone's joy. Murder is a terrible thing, but so is having hatred in your heart towards someone. Destroying someone's property is not good but destroying someone's faith by the way you're living in His name is far worse. You were baptized into His family, so you now are a representative of His great name in everything you do, everything you say, and everywhere you go. Instead of living like the devil and sowing more bad in the world, let's start representing His name.

Football players often have the team's name on the front of their jerseys and their names on the back. The back name is who they go by, but the front name is who they are representing and playing for. You have a name, but you are now representing Him. Play for the name on the front of the jersey and not the back. I know that I must do better at this myself, but I challenge other believers to do the same. Pray this today.

> Search me, O God, and know my heart; test me and know my anxious thoughts. Point out anything in me that offends you and lead me along the path of everlasting life. (Psalms 139:23–24 NLT)

DAY 18

When Pharaoh finally let the people go, God did not lead them along the main road that runs through Philistine territory, even though that was the shortest route to the Promised Land. God said, "If the people are faced with a battle, they might change their minds and return to Egypt." So, God led them in a roundabout way through the wilderness toward the Red Sea. Thus, the Israelites left Egypt like an army ready for battle. (Exodus 13:17–18 NLT)

When you decided to surrender your life to God, it started the journey to the Promised Land—one way of life transformed into another. Yes, there might seem like there's a quicker way to change, but God has a better plan. That quicker way would destroy your faith and frustrate you. He must renew your mind to a new way of life. Salvation isn't just a one-time prayer; it's a new way of life. It is an ongoing transformation. There will be giants to face and new people to meet. Your soul needs to be prepared for everything that stands in your way. By the time you get through the Red Sea, you will be like an army ready for battle—part of the remnant of the last days. If you have seen any of the news, then you know the enemy is coming out with all sorts of fear tactics and agendas. I believe God will use that remnant to keep hope alive for all of those who are losing hope during the hard times.

Remember, just because you don't understand exactly the way God is leading you, stay the course. Trust the One guiding you. Don't put your trust in your eyes because they can cause you to fear. The way the path looks around you is not indicative of His plans. He knows the plans for you. You, however, don't always know. I truly believe the words He spoke to the Israelites through the prophet Jeremiah are also for you today.

> "For I know the plans I have for you," says the Lord. "They are plans for good and not for disaster, to give you a future and a hope." (Jeremiah 29:11 NLT)

DAY 19

The Lord is my strength and my song; he has given me victory. This is my God, and I will praise him— my father's God, and I will exalt him! (Exodus 15:2 NLT)

If you allow the Lord to become the strength that you need, He will give you a victory song to sing too. How do you allow the Lord to become your strength? You do this by faith and obedience to His Word. Moses received instructions from the Lord, and He did exactly what the Lord said.

> Then the Lord gave these instructions to Moses. (Exodus 14:1 NLT)

That's how you get through the Red Sea moments of your life. Trust Him completely and walk through by faith. Just because it looks impossible to change your life doesn't really mean it is. Maybe your new song will be something like this excerpt from Andrew Ripp's song "Roses.".

He must've known about the heartbreak long before us

> He must've known about the mistakes, still He chose us

> Planted the tree where He would die

> Put thorns down the vine, and then He wore them

> And love is the blood red stain, the beauty that the pain exposes

Maybe that's why God made roses

And just like petals falling to the ground

We fall in to the one who's resurrection's here and now[1]

Maybe that's why God decided to make roses. Just because there are some thorns, doesn't mean they aren't still beautiful. The Red Sea doesn't mean the end; rather, it's a new beginning.

[1] Andrew Ripp, "Roses," *Evergreen*, Andrew Ripp Music, 2021.

DAY 20

Trust in the Lord with all your heart and lean not on your own understanding; In all your ways acknowledge Him, And He shall direct your paths. (Proverbs 3:5–6 NKJV)

Everyone needs a life verse to have in his or her heart. This should be a verse that will always be with you no matter what is going on in your life. It should be a verse that can carry you through those hard times, a verse that will always give you hope when you are feeling hopeless, and a verse that sticks with you. If you don't have a verse like this, then you can have mine. This is one of the first verses that I ever memorized. It has stuck with me. It has always helped me get through tough times. I used this verse when I officiated the funeral of my friend's son, who died unexpectedly. I used this verse when I spoke to my sister after getting the news my brother-in-law was killed in a tragic boating accident. I also use this verse whenever I am facing a crossroads in my life and must make a difficult decision. This verse contains the best advice I will ever get in my life.

Can you trust in the Lord with all your heart? Circumstances shouldn't derail that trust in the Lord. Whenever you go out to start your car, do you always trust that it will start? How much more can you trust God in everything you do? Acknowledging Him is one of the best ways to put that trust in Him. Wake up in the morning and thank Him for everything good. Do you have anxiety? Acknowledge Him by applying His word to that anxiety. Also don't always try to understand everything that is happening. That can cause anxiety, depression, frustration, and sleepless nights. Trust that He has you. Acknowledge Him every day. Lean on His words and not on your own understanding of things. He will direct you through this life. That I know. Quit listening to the senseless chatter or any put-downs from other people. God loves you and He is for you. When life isn't good, He still is. Trust—it all comes down to that.

DAY 21

Then Jesus said, "Come to me, all of you who are weary and carry heavy burdens, and I will give you rest. Take my yoke upon you. Let me teach you, because I am humble and gentle at heart, and you will find rest for your souls. For my yoke is easy to bear, and the burden I give you is light." (Matthew 11:28–30 NLT)

This is a very powerful statement coming from Jesus. I know that we can grow weary sometimes. Here we get an invitation to take everything that's burdensome and wearing us down to Him, exchanging our heavy yoke for His lighter one. That's the love of God! That's His amazing grace on display in our lives. It can be hard to let that heavy yoke go because it can become so familiar to us, and letting it go to God seems like we are losing control. By getting to know God better, you will start to trust Him more. Get alone with God on a daily basis, even if you don't really feel like doing anything at all. Getting to know your Heavenly Father is the best thing you can do for your heart. It will become so full of joy that it will start to overflow to everyone else around you. Don't let the enemy or the cares of the world put that heaviness on you. Trust Him with everything instead.

DAY 22

"Don't let your hearts be troubled. Trust in God, and trust also in me…I am leaving you with a gift—peace of mind and heart. And the peace I give is a gift the world cannot give. So don't be troubled or afraid." (John 14:1, 27 NLT)

Jesus is about to be crucified and He tells the disciples not to let their hearts be troubled. The very person who is about to go through unimaginable pain is telling everyone this. He had His heart aligned with the Father's and He knew that on the other side of the suffering would be the glory. He also knows that the disciples would be extremely anxious because the very person they gave up everything to follow was about to die. If they looked only at the circumstances, it would look hopeless. Did they give up everything for no reason? He tells them that He will give them a peace that nothing in this world can ever give them. They would need to have faith regardless of how everything looks in the natural. The same can be true for us today. The circumstances are the facts, but don't let your heart be troubled because the truth found in God's word is greater than any facts. He will give you a peace that no drug, drink, or person can ever do. Get your heart aligned with God's by accepting Jesus into yours. Then you can look at everything through the eyes of faith instead of the eyes of the body. God's plan and God's purpose have seen you through it all.

DAY 23

❖◆❖◆❖◆❖

Then the Lord God called to the man, "Where are you?" (Genesis 3:9 NLT)

Why did God ask Adam where he was? God already knew that. God saw right where Adam was at that point in his life. God sees you right where you are at too. He knows everything that has happened to you and the place that you're in right now. The reason he asked that question was to get Adam to confess to Him where he was. God sees you but He is waiting for you to turn to Him. You're at a place in your life and you might not know what to do next. You don't even know how you ended up in this mess or why you started down this ugly road, thinking, *How did I end up where I am?* Adam hid because he felt ashamed of what he had done. Maybe you are ashamed of your past choices too. You may feel guilty about some decisions you made, and you are scared about the future. God sees you and will meet you right where you are. Confess everything to Him. Ask for forgiveness. Accept Jesus into your heart and turn from the old way of life. You can be real with God. He can work with what's real. Shame will always be a result of disobedience to God. Quit hiding from Him. Quit running away from Him. He sees you and is calling your name. There is a better way and it's not too late for you. You have breath and a heartbeat. That means you still have hope.

"Where are you?" That's the question. Connect with God and get your heart aligned with His.

DAY 24

"I will send terror ahead of you to drive out the Hivites, Canaanites, and Hittites. But I will not drive them out in a single year, because the land would become desolate, and the wild animals would multiply and threaten you. I will drive them out a little at a time until your population has increased enough to take possession of the land." (Exodus 23:28–30 NLT)

We always want everything to happen quickly. This microwave society we live in is always rushing everything. I have personally found that being transformed into the person God wants me to be is taking time. My spirit was instantly made new, but my soul is being renewed daily. My spirit man was born again, but my soul (mind, will, and emotions) must be renewed by the Word of God. God will make the way for you, but it will usually be one step at time. I believe that is so that we will be more likely to stay the course and not be overwhelmed by all the changes. God wants to save us, heal us, and equip us to be lights for others' darkness. Make a difference in this world for His purpose—one step at a time, one day a time, one prayer at a time, and defeating one giant at a time. You can do this. I believe in you. More importantly, God believes in you. Trust His ways.

DAY 25

❖◆◆◆◆◆◆ ❖

> Don't copy the behavior and customs of this world,
> but let God transform you into a new person by
> changing the way you think. Then you will learn
> to know God's will for you, which is good and
> pleasing and perfect. (Romans 12:2 NLT)

The caterpillar goes through a transformation process during its life. It starts out a little bit ugly. Then after a while, it goes into the darkness of the cocoon. It's dark and lonely inside the cocoon. That's exactly where a lot of you find yourselves right now. Your life has started out a little ugly and now you find yourself in the darkness of a jail cell. Being in that position can feel quite lonely. Being separated from your family and friends is hard. Facing an unknown future can make everything seem even darker. It isn't looking good, but while the caterpillar is in the darkness, God does the greatest work in its life, transforming it through a process into a beautiful butterfly. Now it's extremely beautiful and able to do something it couldn't do before—now it can fly! It became something totally different.

That is exactly what God can do for your life too. While in the darkness of jail, God can begin to work on your heart. You are sober now, not distracted by the world, and you are in a quieter place for Him to start speaking clearly to you. You can have your life completely transformed while you're in there. It's not the end of your life, but it's the beginning of a beautiful life. Like the butterfly developing wings, God will develop you. Now you can do some things that you never could do before. The darkness might be a scary place in your life but seek God through it. You can leave jail a much better person than when you went in. That's what God can do. No matter what your past is like, it's up to you to make the decision to seek Him.

"Today I have given you the choice between life and death, between blessings and curses. Now I call on heaven and earth to witness the choice you make. Oh, that you would choose life, so that you and your descendants might live!" (Deuteronomy 30:19 NLT)

DAY 26

Late that night, the disciples were in their boat in the middle of the lake, and Jesus was alone on land. He saw that they were in serious trouble, rowing hard and struggling against the wind and waves. About three o'clock in the morning Jesus came toward them, walking on the water. He intended to go past them, but when they saw him walking on the water, they cried out in terror, thinking he was a ghost. They were all terrified when they saw him. But Jesus spoke to them at once. "Don't be afraid," he said. "Take courage! I am here!" (Mark 6:47–50 NLT)

In Mark's account of this incident, we see that the disciples were out in the boat without Jesus, and they were struggling against the wind. Isn't that a beautiful picture of most of us in life? We just finish spending time with Jesus, but we go out into the world and the enemy starts to put up resistance against us. We strain and struggle to overcome but only wear ourselves out, letting all the cares and concerns prevent us from getting anywhere. We become exhausted, anxious, feel hopeless, and even become sick. As soon as the resistance comes, we immediately open the doors of our hearts to the enemy instead of trusting what God has already told us. When we can't see Jesus in the boat with us, we let fear in. He is there. He is always there. He won't ever leave us or forsake us. There he was walking towards them, but it was hard for them to recognize Him because it can be hard to recognize someone in the storms of life. Their eyes were blurred by the tears. Their clarity was clouded because of fear. He is always there!

We can see want happens when someone lets Jesus into his or her life. They hear, "Take courage! It is I. Don't be afraid." Then He climbs into their boat and the wind dies down. The winds of life won't go away completely, but they will die down. The struggle to the other side will become less difficult. The wind won't be the problem anymore; the only problem will be ourselves. Next, we will look at how Matthew explains what Peter did. Guard your heart. Trust Him. He is there. He always will be there.

DAY 27

Where there is no vision, the people perish: But he that keepeth the law, happy is he. (Proverbs 29:18 KJV)

I know that I often don't know where I want to go in life. That leads to frustration and uncertainty about every decision. You come to a place in your life that requires a decision. It is a crossroads that will lead you to where you need to go, but without a vision in your heart from God, which one you pick won't really matter. Maybe that vision could be to earn a degree, build a business, adopt a child, or go on a mission trip somewhere. It could be any goal that would require God's divine guidance and that will be a blessing to others. Without a vision your life is just perishing. You need that vision in your heart. It gives you passion and purpose. It becomes your *why*. Why do you get up every day? Why are you praying so earnestly? Why are you so motivated? It's important to have that in your life. It gives you a fire for life. It will have you working closely with God for that divine guide and wisdom.

There will be times that you will get tired, and God will renew your strength. Without that vision from God, every decision will only lead to frustration, anxiety, and a lot of confusion. You come to a crossroads and need to decide which way your life should go. You can't ever decide. You change your mind often. You start one way and then just quit when the voice of enemy starts chatting in your ear. It is extremely frustrating and will leave you feeling stuck.

In Lewis Carroll's *Alice's Adventures in* Wonderland, the Cheshire Cat tries to tell Alice the truth about direction in life.

[Alice asked], "Would you tell me, please, which way I ought to go from here?"

"That depends a good deal on where you want to get to," said the Cat.

"I don't much care where—" said Alice.

"Then it doesn't much matter which way you go," said the Cat.

"—so long as I get *somewhere*," said Alice.

"Oh, you're sure to do that," said the Cat, "if only you walk long enough."[2]

You will always end up somewhere, but it won't be where God is trying to guide you to. Get that vision in your heart. Lean on God every step of the way. Then when those crossroads of life come up, you will know which road to take.

This is what the Lord says: "Stop at the crossroads and look around. Ask for the old, godly way, and walk in it. Travel its path, and you will find rest for your souls." But you reply, "No, that's not the road we want!" (Jeremiah 6:16 NLT)

---

[2] Lewis Carroll, *Alice's Adventures in Wonderland*, Project Gutenberg, last modified October 12, 2020, https://www.gutenberg.org/files/11/11-h/11-h.htm

DAY 28

On another Sabbath day, a man with a deformed right hand was in the synagogue while Jesus was teaching. The teachers of religious law and the Pharisees watched Jesus closely. If he healed the man's hand, they planned to accuse him of working on the Sabbath. But Jesus knew their thoughts. He said to the man with the deformed hand, "Come and stand in front of everyone." So, the man came forward. Then Jesus said to his critics, "I have a question for you. Does the law permit good deeds on the Sabbath, or is it a day for doing evil? Is this a day to save life or to destroy it?" He looked around at them one by one and then said to the man, "Hold out your hand." So, the man held out his hand, and it was restored! At this, the enemies of Jesus were wild with rage and began to discuss what to do with him. (Luke 6:6–11 NLT)

In the passage above, everyone is focused on everything Jesus did. There's nothing wrong with that, but I want you to look at what the guy with the deformed hand did. This guy is a lot like most of us. We go to church and stick out our good hands—the hands that everyone sees. We go around shaking hands with our good hands while hiding the deformed hands so no one will notice it. We lift one of our arms up to praise God so our good hands will be out, but we hide our deformed ones so no one around us can see it. We go to church and act like everything is just fine. Then when we leave, we secretly struggle with something. We pray for God's healing, but we are always hiding the deformity.

This man was vulnerable before Jesus and the rest of the congregation. By faith, he stuck out his deformed hand toward Jesus. God can't heal what you continue to hide. You have been going to church for a while but still can't shake that addiction? Be vulnerable before God and stick out the addiction by faith. Maybe go to treatment if you need to and bring it up to your small group so you can have that support system around you. Whatever you are hiding from God that is continuing to block you from being healed is your deformed hand. Once this man was obedient to the words of Jesus and stuck his bad hand toward Him, he was healed! Whatever is hindering or hurting you, by faith stick it out towards God and deal with it. Let Him heal the hurts, break the addiction, and truly set you free. Everyone around you will also see the power of God at work and will want what you just received. God can heal anything that you are willing to set in front of Him. Be physically, spiritually, and emotionally set free in the name of Jesus! Amen.

> He personally carried our sins in his body on the cross so that we can be dead to sin and live for what is right. By his wounds you are healed. (1 Peter 2:24 NLT)

DAY 29

Dear brothers and sisters, when troubles of any kind come your way, consider it an opportunity for great joy. For you know that when your faith is tested, your endurance has a chance to grow. So let it grow, for when your endurance is fully developed, you will be perfect and complete, needing nothing. (James 1:2–4 NLT)

I have trained for and run a couple of marathons. I know a little bit about having enough endurance to run to the end of 26.2 miles. I don't think it was just a coincidence that when I started running, God started working on my heart. He was able to get me alone and away from the noise. I was also completely sober at that time. My mind was clear, but I still didn't know God yet. The training wasn't always easy, and I had a few days where I thought about quitting completely. I also started with some 5Ks and half marathons before I ever tried the 26.2 miles.

Running is a lot like the journey many of you might be on right now. God is working on your heart, and you are finally ready to start this run with Him. Now comes the training and testing of your endurance. There will always be obstacles and difficulties that tempt you to quit. The enemy doesn't want you to run the race that God has set before you. You will have several different types of workouts too: short runs, long runs, faster paced runs, cross training, and strength training. All will serve to help you run the race. You will face hills and the elements of the outdoors. What you consume will also be a big factor in finishing strong.

All of that will be just like your race (life) with God. You will be trained and equipped for a purpose. You will face some ups and downs. The elements you are in (environment) won't always be perfect. There will be days when you don't feel like loving your neighbor, but by faith you do it anyway. There will be days you would rather stay in bed than go to church. Then you get up and go anyway. There will be times you will want to quit your job. Maybe God is telling you that it's not about you getting out, but you are there to get Him in. You battle a sickness or injury, but you continue to praise God through it. You get up every day and get into the word. You pray your way through the tough days, and you thank God always. Is it always easy? Absolutely not, but each time you face troubles, you build up the endurance you need. When it comes time to finish the hardest part of the run, those last 6.2 miles, you will be ready. You have already done the work and ran the shorter runs as tests. You know how to run, and you consumed good foods.

David faced the lion and the bear before he took out Goliath. He had the faith for the fight and the endurance to keep the faith going forward. Don't get all upset when life gets hard. Thank God for His grace and goodness. He didn't bring you this far to leave you. You are building up to something special. It looks hard and you feel overwhelmed at times. I get that. I understand that. You need to keep the faith through it all. Look at what Paul says: "For I can do everything through Christ, who gives me strength" (Philippians 4:13 NLT).

Keep running the race God has set before you. Don't look back. Don't give up. Stay the course. You already know there's a beautiful finish line ahead, so just keep going, and inspire other runners along the way.

> He gives power to the weak and strength to the powerless. Even youths will become weak and tired, and young men will fall in exhaustion. But those who trust in the Lord will find new strength. They will soar high on wings like eagles. They will run and not grow weary. They will walk and not faint. (Isaiah 40:29–31 NLT)

DAY 30

❖◆◆◆◆◆❖

Guard your heart above all else, for it determines
the course of your life. (Proverbs 4:23 NLT)

I wanted to share something that I had recently learned. I had this
scripture dropped into my heart while I was praying. I learned that
a person can't carry the weight of uncontrollable situations around
in his or her heart. Doing so will start to infect you with the enemy's
poison. It will make you sick, irritated, anxious, and depressed, and
leave you stuck in frustration. It's better to just step to the side and
let God do His job. God's Word is absolute truth, and you can trust
Him no matter what. You need to keep your heart guarded from
the attack of the enemy. He will try to hit your heart and steer you
off course. This will affect everything you do: how you treat other
people, how you work, how you study, how you think, how much
peace you have, and how healthy you are.

DAY 31

Let all that I am praise the Lord; with my whole heart, I will praise his holy name. Let all that I am praise the Lord; may I never forget the good things he does for me. (Psalms 103:1–2 NLT)

What does it mean to praise the Lord with your whole heart? How can a person even do that when the world is such a mess? Turn on the television or scroll through your social media account. You will see news about another person missing, or another mass shooting that has taken place somewhere. The vaccine and COVID are sure to be among the top news stories of the day. How can you praise the Lord with all that negative information trying to infect your heart daily? In verse 2 above, you can see how David did that. He doesn't forget all the good things God does for him. God is good even when life isn't. That statement is absolutely the truth.

2020 was a crazy year for almost everyone. Everyone had the COVID chaos to deal with, but a lot of other hard stuff seemed to come along too. How do you praise Him will all that going on? You do it by faith. Your faith isn't in the circumstances you are going through but in a God who is always good. He never changes. To worship with your whole heart is to give God your best. You lift your hands up because He is faithful. You lift your voice up because He is good. You serve others because He is love. You give because He is a provider. All your heart goes into worshiping Him because there's nothing impossible with God. Everything you do starts in your heart, and you need to get out of your own head so you can truly connect with God. That's where the connection is made—in your heart. Then you can make your thoughts line up with your heart. Don't let life drag you under your circumstances. Let your life overcome every circumstance. Jesus listed the heart first for a reason.

> Jesus replied, "You must love the Lord your God with all your heart, all your soul, and all your mind." (Matthew 22:37 NLT)

I know it hurts now, but you need to lift up that broken hallelujah out of your heart. I know it looks impossible now, but God is able. I know your head has doubts, but you do it by faith anyway. It's a matter of the heart. That's where your faith is. You are going to be okay. He is so good.

DAY 32

"Study this Book of Instruction continually. Meditate on it day and night so you will be sure to obey everything written in it. Only then will you prosper and succeed in all you do." (Joshua 1:8 NLT)

People are often on fire for God initially, but then after a while that fire starts to dwindle. Then eventually the fire goes out completely and they start reverting to their old ways. How does this happen? I believe this scripture tells us how it happens. People become lazy and complacent. They don't study anymore. Praying becomes a thing of the past. Applying God's word to daily life slowly starts to stop. In layman's terms, people quit putting wood on the fire. We need to stay focused on God day and night, studying, praying, and applying. Otherwise, that passionate fire will be extinguished by the ways of the world. The enemy can't put God's fire out, but he can get you to.

What are some subtle ways this happens? Our favorite football teams become the best in the country. We start watching ESPN instead of studying. We start praising touchdowns instead of God. We read the scoreboards more than His Word. People know that we are fans, but not Christians. There is nothing wrong with football. It's my favorite sport and I follow along with it too. I noticed that it could take over some of a person's time. The person schedules time to watch the game but misses out on time with his or her spouse.

Another example is a bad report on something. The doctor gives you a bad medical report. You start to meditate on those words instead of God's words. Thinking on everything bad instead of what God has already said will put your fire out. Then suddenly, your words are negative and your actions towards everyone change too.

You used to talk about faith, but when it's time to walk by faith, you stop. Then your faith is pointed in the wrong direction. You need to be focused on God all the time, otherwise your focus will become blurry over time. The enemy will try to get you with a slow fade, a little bit at a time. One drink here becomes okay, or maybe it is just one pill to get through the day. You decide you can skip your devotional time today. It's only one day. You feel too tired to pray because the game went into overtime. It is a slow fade. The next thing you know, life is different. You are broke and busted, in jail or maybe the hospital. Then you ask God what He is doing, when it was you who turned from Him. God is blamed a lot for the slow fade, but it's never Him that changes.

Jesus Christ is the same yesterday, today, and forever.
(Hebrews 13:8 NLT)

Study, pray, and apply. It's a daily walk with God, not a walk once a week. Once a week will start that slow fade. Throw some wood on the fire and make it burn forever.

DAY 33

My enemy has chased me. He has knocked me
to the ground and forces me to live in darkness
like those in the grave. I am losing all hope; I am
paralyzed with fear. I remember the days of old. I
ponder all your great works and think about what
you have done. I lift my hands to you in prayer.
I thirst for you as parched land thirsts for rain.
(Psalms 143:3–6 NLT)

Have you ever had the enemy chase after you, knock you down, force
you to live in a dark place, and leave you feeling hopeless and thinking
that that dark place is forever? You are paralyzed by fear and not able to
do some of the things that you used to do. The psalmist in this writing
can relate to that. Whatever you are currently going through can be like
what he was dealing with. Maybe it was the loss of a loved one. It could
be anxiety hitting you for some unknown reason, dealing with a health
concern, or even witnessing a loved one struggle through life—whatever
the enemy might be knocking you down with and using to force you to
live in the darkness of depression. Here the psalmist shows us what we
can do during these times. He advises us to remember the days of old
and ponder what God has already done in our lives. He lifts his hands
in prayer despite everything that's happening. He knows that God will
satisfy the thirst when his life is dehydrated. The only way to keep from
getting stuck like that is to make a move toward God. It is not always
easy to do, but that's what I am trying to encourage you to do today.

In your unfailing love, silence all my enemies and
destroy all my foes, for I am your servant. (Psalms
143:12 NLT)

DAY 34

❖◆❖◆❖

"I have told you all this so that you may have peace
in me. Here on earth, you will have many trials and
sorrows. But take heart, because I have overcome
the world." (John 16:33 NLT)

The world was supposed to be a paradise, but we messed that up.
God has a plan, but the world around us is heading in the wrong
direction. The enemy wants you to follow that way too. The worldly
ways will tell you that your life can never be better. God's words say
that He has a good plan for your life.

"For I know the plans I have for you," says the Lord.
"They are plans for good and not for disaster, to give
you a future and a hope." (Jeremiah 29:11 NLT)

The world will tell you that you need a bunch of medicine
to get through the anxiety this world is bringing on you. Take
one medication and then another because the first one isn't doing
enough. Then take another one for the side effects. Then take another
one because you might need this too. I am not against medication,
just against overmedicating. God's word says,

Be anxious for nothing, but in everything by prayer
and supplication, with thanksgiving, let your
requests be made known to God; and the peace
of God, which surpasses all understanding, will
guard your hearts and minds through Christ Jesus.
(Philippians 4:6–7 NKJV)

I know life can be very difficult at times, but God says that you can have a supernatural peace while you are here on the Earth. That type of peace won't come from any pills, powders, potions, or people. It only comes from aligning your heart with His. I know it's easier to turn to a bottle. It's tangible, it's acceptable, it's accessible, and it will numb you. That's what everyone wants: to feel good and have a good time. The problem is that that way is short-lived and you're letting substances become your god. They bring you under the influence, and that's demonic. You end up doing and saying things that you normally wouldn't, leading to a lot of trouble. In addition, the more you rely on a substance, the more you will need. The good stuff in your life will start to die. Prescription medicines are okay for a while and have their place, but a bunch of them isn't good. Taking them without seek the Lord will also lead to needing higher doses and more of them.

I have been there too. I know what anxiety and depression will do to a person. I am also aware of how the world treats it. The enemy offers an apple. It looks good and it tastes good. The problem is that it isn't good. It's a bad apple and you can't see it because the poison is at the core. You digest it and now you open the door to the enemy. Other people can help you get through life, but they can't do what God can. You need the Holy Spirit to help you discern their advice. Job got some bad advice from well-meaning friends. You need godly people in your life but remember that God should be your main source. God is good even when life isn't. Keep the faith through the hard times and you will see His goodness. There is nothing better than the peace that God gives. Pray about it today.

DAY 35

"But when I am afraid, I will put my trust in you."
(Psalms 56:3 NLT)

I used to always think that fear and faith could not co-exist. That hasn't been the truth in my life. I have never done anything that God has called me to and not been afraid. Faith is not the absence of fear but moving forward despite being afraid. The psalmist says in this scripture, when I am afraid, I will put my trust in you. Even with those feelings of fear, put your trust in God. Move forward by faith and trust that He will walk with you. If you feel that He is calling you to something that seems impossible for someone like you, then I would venture to say that He is. Take a step toward that and you will get confirmation along the way. Writing a devotional seemed too big for me, and it is. I had to rely on the prompts of the Holy Spirit to do it. I simply said yes and started walking forward. Pray about it. Get that vision in your heart. Then take a step toward that goal by faith despite feeling afraid. The world needs what God has put inside of you. Teacher, preacher, running a marathon, police officer or whatever is put on your heart. There is a bigger purpose behind it. It will positively impact others and inspire them to overcome their fears too.

DAY 36

⟡✦◆✦◆✦◆✦⟡

Then, calling the crowd to join his disciples, he said, "If any of you wants to be my follower, you must give up your own way, take up your cross, and follow me. If you try to hang on to your life, you will lose it. But if you give up your life for my sake and for the sake of the Good News, you will save it. And what do you benefit if you gain the whole world but lose your own soul?" (Mark 8:34–36 NLT)

Maybe you are dealing with an addiction and are really struggling to find ways to get through it. I am here to tell you that you can get through it, and there is a much better way to live your life. The first thing you really need to do is be open and honest. Admit that you have a problem with addiction and that it's a struggle for you. It's not a sign of weakness. It is a sign that you need Jesus in your life. Admitting everything to God is the first step. Step two is to ask God to help give you the strength to overcome the addiction. You admitted the problem and you invited God into your life. Now you are ready to follow the example of Jesus and overcome it. Your spirit is ready and now you will need to renew your soul (mind, will, and emotions) to a new way of life. The spirit is made new, the soul can be renewed by the word of God, but the flesh (body) will do everything it can to give into the temptations of those old desires. You will have the spiritual strength to get through this. The battle will be taking place between your soul and body. You will have to take up your cross and crucify that old way of life. Your heart (spirit) has the strength to do this.

You now need to make the necessary changes to your life and

renew your mind to the ways of God. Will it be easy? Probably not at first, but that fleshly desire will eventually be crucified. New desires will fill your heart, like a desire to study His Word. The enemy will be in your ear a lot because following Jesus isn't what he wants. If you do decide to hang onto the old ways, you will eventually go back to them. When you give up that old way of life for God's way, you will save your life, both on earth and in eternity. Don't lose your soul (mind) to gain anything from this world. Refuse to lose. You are strong enough. You are equipped. You are prepared. You are ready to be free. Take it one day at a time. You can do this.

DAY 37

After consulting the people, the king appointed singers to walk ahead of the army, singing to the Lord and praising him for his holy splendor. This is what they sang: "Give thanks to the Lord; his faithful love endures forever!" At the very moment they began to sing and give praise, the Lord caused the armies of Ammon, Moab, and Mount Seir to start fighting among themselves. (2 Chronicles 20:21–22 NLT)

The king had three different enemies attacking him at the same time. Ammon, Moab, and Mount Seir were all coming at him. You might find yourself in a similar situation, with more than one enemy coming at you at the same time. These could be the wickedness of the world, the devil, and your own past mistakes which continue to haunt your thoughts. Anxiety and fear overwhelm you. Look at what the king did when he first heard about the attackers that were coming.

Alarmed, Jehoshaphat resolved to inquire of the Lord, and he proclaimed a fast for all Judah. (2 Chronicles 20:3 NIV)

The anxiety and fear alarmed him that this was a big problem, so he inquired of the Lord. That's what we should all do as soon as the alarms go off. Anxiety and fear are alarms for us to inquire of the Lord. The answer the king got didn't really make much sense. He sent the singers out ahead of the army. That's not who would normally be on the frontlines of the battle. The king did what the Lord said.

Do you see the application you can take for your life? You made a mistake in the past. You feel guilty for that. Now you find yourself in a jail cell and people are coming at you. On top of everything, the devil is chattering in your ear trying to get you to give up on life. That sets off the anxiety and fear. The alarm is going off. Ask the Lord about everything, then by faith praise Him! Praise brings God's power to the problems. The praise team went out before the army, and the enemies started to attack each other instead of the king. It confused the enemy because it brought God into the fight. The battle belongs to the Lord. The army didn't even need to fight.

I know you are in a bad place. I know life is hard. King Jehoshaphat was in a tough place too. He had an entire country to protect. It wasn't just about him. Your decision to completely trust God through this and by faith praise Him won't be just about you. Your kids and family are your country to protect. By faith, Joshua walked and worshiped around the walls of Jericho. Walk in the obedience to the word and worship regardless of what you can physically see. The battle belongs to the Lord. You will get through this mess. There are better days ahead. God is good even when life isn't.

> So, Jehoshaphat's kingdom was at peace, for his God had given him rest on every side. (2 Chronicles 20:30 NLT)

DAY 38

Dear brothers and sisters, when troubles of any kind
come your way, consider it an opportunity for great
joy. (James 1:2 NLT)

Troubles are opportunities for great joy. James, are you serious right
now? Someone is saying right now, "James, you don't even know
what I am going through. If it was a smaller issue, then maybe I
could still have great joy. When I get through this, then I can have
that type James is writing about." Why is this even in the Bible? How
can a person apply this scripture in a life that has so much darkness?
I will tell you how I do it. I pour a cup of coffee, turn on some music,
read through the Bible, and pray through it. Great joy comes because
the troubles let me know that I am still alive, and that God is still
good despite everything. Plus, it always pushes me closer to God.

When darkness comes upon you, praise Him anyway! Pour a cup
of coffee, listen for your song to come on, search the scriptures, and
pray about it more than you talk to people about it. You are either
going through something, just went through something, or will
be going through something. All are opportunities for joy because
God's presence in our life isn't conditional and everything will work
out if you will continue seeking Him. His plan, His purpose, and
His peace are all good because He is.

And we know that God causes everything to work
together for the good of those who love God and are
called according to his purpose for them. (Romans
8:28 NLT)

DAY 39

❖✦◆✦◆✦❖

"'The Lord your God is going ahead of you. He will fight for you, just as you saw him do in Egypt. And you saw how the Lord your God cared for you all along the way as you traveled through the wilderness, just as a father cares for his child. Now he has brought you to this place.'" (Deuteronomy 1:30–31 NLT)

Moses told the Israelites not to be afraid of the giants in the Promised Land. He said that God would go ahead of them and would fight for them. He also reminded them of everything God had already done and how He was with them as they traveled. Now He had brought the Israelites to this place. Maybe that is where you find yourself: this place, a place in your life where you either trust what God has placed in your heart, or you don't. He has brought you this far and now you know about the giants that are in the way.

I can tell you that I have come to a this place moment in my life a few times. I often have done exactly what the Israelites did too. They complained and didn't trust God. That kept them from moving forward into the Promised Land.

You can't live the plans God has for you that way. We come to that place in our life, and we let the fears and uncertainty direct us instead of the Holy Spirit. It happens to me almost every single time God brings me to that place. How much better do we have it than the Israelites did at that point? Not only do we have God's written words, but we have the Holy Spirit within us. God isn't just with us but within us, giving us a power that they didn't have. Have you accepted Jesus into your heart and been baptized in His name? Ask the Holy Spirit to fill you the next time God brings you to that place.

Face those giants by faith and go forward even if you feel afraid. Maybe you are sitting in jail right now—that is your *that place* moment. Are you going to trust God from now on with your life or are you going to complain about everything you currently see? Trust His word and ways or you can start complaining about everything that you are going through. One way will seem right and feel good to your flesh. The other way will seem hard and impossible. Which way do you think God wants to take you?

> There is a path before each person that seems right,
> but it ends in death. (Proverbs 14:12 NLT)

Go back to your old ways and things in your life will start to die. It's the price we pay for going against God's way. God has already paid the price for your life to be different. He gave you Jesus.

> For the wages of sin is death, but the free gift of
> God is eternal life through Christ Jesus our Lord.
> (Romans 6:23 NLT)

That place isn't a place to quit or stop at forever. It's a place where your heart is changed, and your faith becomes active.

DAY 40

Then the word of the Lord came to Elijah: "Leave here, turn eastward and hide in the Kerith Ravine, east of the Jordan. You will drink from the brook, and I have directed the ravens to supply you with food there." So, he did what the Lord had told him. He went to the Kerith Ravine, east of the Jordan, and stayed there. The ravens brought him bread and meat in the morning and bread and meat in the evening, and he drank from the brook. (1 Kings 17:2–6 NIV)

Let's talk about a place called *there*. The word of the Lord came to Elijah and he was given instructions that he needed to follow. God had a plan and a purpose for Elijah, just like He does for you. Maybe God has placed something on your heart that you have previously blown off. Maybe it's to pursue something in the ministry full time, write a book, be a teacher, or open your own local business. Whatever God has on your heart to pursue, it won't go away no matter how much you ignore it. In the natural, it looks impossible, and you have no idea how you would be able to afford it. Elijah got a word from the Lord to go in a certain direction. When he followed the directions, he would be provided for when he got there. The brook would be there for him to drink from, and the ravens would feed him when he got there—a place called there. When he got there, God provided what Elijah needed.

When you start walking by faith towards what God is calling you to, you will His supernatural provisions in your life. You must start taking some steps of faith and go toward a place called there. Maybe you can't afford to get your book published. Write it by faith and start making some phone calls. Let others read some of it too. Get the word out about it, then trust He will meet you there. Whatever is on your heart, go after it. If it's from God, there will be a burning desire inside of you that won't go away, and it will look nearly impossible to do. On your own, it will be impossible but where God guides, He provides. Start heading to a place called there. When you get there, you will see the goodness of God. Start writing, building, or studying, and take that step of faith. The brook will be there for you to drink from, and the ravens will bring the food to you there. It can be scary, but faith goes forward anyway. Don't let the dreams and desires God put into your heart die. No matter where you are in your life, no matter how old you are, no matter what you have done or what other people think, if you are still alive, that God-dream is still alive too. Go there!

> And my God will meet all your needs according to the riches of his glory in Christ Jesus. (Philippians 4:19 NIV)

DAY 41

—◆◆◆◆◆—

Sometime later the brook dried up because there had been no rain in the land. Then the word of the Lord came to him: "Go at once to Zarephath in the region of Sidon and stay there. I have directed a widow there to supply you with food." (1 Kings 17:7–9 NIV)

A place called there shows up again in the life of Elijah. God had previously directed Elijah to go to a certain place and the provisions would be there. Now the brook that was there for him to drink out of has dried up. God then gives him another word with new directions. There is something I want you to notice about this. God won't give you a new word until you listen to the last word that He gave you. Why would He keep guiding you if you wouldn't move the last time He placed something on your heart? Another thing I want you to notice is that the provisions for that time dried up. That's because it was time for Elijah to move to another place. The comfort that place provided had to be removed so he wouldn't stay there.

How often does God take us to new place in our lives but we stay where we are because it's comfortable? Sometimes I believe God must make things a little uncomfortable for us so we will seek Him again and be willing to move on to the next thing. Elijah was told that a widow would be there to feed him. He had to go to a place called there again. By faith Elijah obeyed the word of the Lord. Be brave. Be like Elijah. Trust what God's got on your heart and take the next step of faith to a place called there.

DAY 42

❖◆❖◆❖◆❖

> This is the word that came to Jeremiah from the Lord: "Go down to the potter's house, and there I will give you my message." (Jeremiah 18:1–2 NIV)

God gives Jeremiah a word. He tells him to go there, and He would give him a message after he gets there. God reveals to Jeremiah where *there* is in this verse, but He doesn't give him the message yet. If Jeremiah isn't obedient to the first word, then he won't get the second word that God wants to give to him. God had to get Jeremiah in the right place at the right time so Jeremiah could hear the right word. Sometimes God will reveal the place called there to you but not reveal what you are going to do there. He never says what Jeremiah was going to do or what provisions he would need. He just says go to the potter's house.

God doesn't usually reveal the entire plan to us at once. That would be overwhelming and cause us to have more doubts. It's one part at a time, one step of faith at a time, and one day at a time. Often, we get so concerned about the steps that might be coming down the road, we get too nervous to obey the word He just put on our hearts. Fear starts contaminating our faith. We need to trust Him through everything. Through all the good, the bad, and the ugly, His plans never change. He knows the plan from beginning to end. We don't and that's to protect us.

> "For I know the plans I have for you," declares the Lord, "plans to prosper you and not to harm you, plans to give you hope and a future." (Jeremiah 29:11 NIV)

DAY 43

But God is my helper. The Lord keeps me alive!
(Psalms 54:4 NLT)

Maybe you are facing some difficult days right now. That's just how this life is sometimes. David had enemies attacking him. They were trying to kill him. David starts off this prayer by telling God what's going on. He doesn't do this because God didn't know, but I believe he wanted to get that junk out of his heart and cast his cares onto the Lord. Then he brings God into his situation with two words that are vital for all believers to have in their prayers: "But God." David is saying, "This is happening to me, but God is my helper. He keeps me going. He keeps my hopes and dreams alive! I am dealing with this setback, but God. I know this situation looks impossible, but God." Maybe you can say, "The doctor's report was bad, but God" or "I am not sure how I will overcome this bad habit, but God." Confess the problem to God so you can get it out of your heart and then trust Him. Say these words to yourself when you start to feel afraid or have that hopeless feeling that anxiety often brings on. But God. Say it, shout it, or even sing it. Just declare to the devil that God is your helper.

DAY 44

The Lord gave this message to Jonah son of Amittai:
"Get up and go to the great city of Nineveh.
Announce my judgment against it because I have
seen how wicked its people are." But Jonah got up
and went in the opposite direction to get away from
the Lord. He went down to the port of Joppa, where
he found a ship leaving for Tarshish. He bought a
ticket and went on board, hoping to escape from the
Lord by sailing to Tarshish. But the Lord hurled a
powerful wind over the sea, causing a violent storm
that threatened to break the ship apart. (Jonah
1:1–4 NLT)

Jonah got a message from the Lord about a place called there. God
revealed both the place and purpose to him. I believe that's one
reason why God usually doesn't reveal everything to us all at once.
That sent Jonah running in the opposite direction! He didn't want
to go there and do that. Jonah often gets a bad reputation because
of this. Truth is, we all have gone in the opposite direction of God's
plan and purpose for our life. Maybe you find yourself in and out of
jail all the time. That's going in the wrong direction. Maybe you are
struggling with addiction, and you know deep inside that you need
to lay that on the altar. You know that you should be seeking Him
as hard as you seek that substance. Maybe you feel called to preach
but the pastor has you cleaning the church. You get frustrated and
quit doing it. How can you preach when you can't even serve?

Quitting is going in the wrong direction. There are several
decisions that you might have made, and they have you running in
the wrong direction. Jonah even bought a ticket trying to escape.

Trying to avoid God with worldly ways isn't going to work. Jonah's decision brought his storm onto the others around him. Your decisions don't just affect you, but everyone around you will feel the effects too. You keep doing what you are doing, and other people sometimes get hurt. It's never just about you. Jonah's decision to buy a ticket and get on that boat, threatened everything around him. A lot of times, we pray for God to help us get through this situation when in fact the storm was our own fault, and He has been trying to get us turned around this whole time. I suggest that you sit alone with God and start praying for clarity to know how to get back on track and what you need to do next. Stay with that prayer and be ready to obey what He places on your heart.

DAY 45

Fearing for their lives, the desperate sailors shouted to their gods for help and threw the cargo overboard to lighten the ship. But all this time Jonah was sound asleep down in the hold. So, the captain went down after him. "How can you sleep at a time like this?" he shouted. "Get up and pray to your god! Maybe he will pay attention to us and spare our lives." (Jonah 1:5–6 NLT)

God tells Jonah where there actually is and what his purpose will be. Then next thing we read about is Jonah running away from His calling. This brings on a storm, affecting everyone around him. Sometimes the storm is a direct result of our own disobedience because we continued living life the way we felt like, and because we were led by our feelings rather than faith in God. As you read in today's scripture, everyone started to become fearful. They turned to their gods for help. They also started to battle this demonic storm by throwing things overboard. There is nothing they could have done.

How often do we try our gods to get through a storm like this? We continue on our own paths, going in the opposite direction of God's calling for us, and it stirs up a violent anxiety storm within us. That storm goes everywhere with us, so we cry out to other gods: strong anxiety meds, hard liquor to deaden our senses, the pleasure of sexual partners to numb the hurt, or whatever else we turn to instead of God Almighty. The god of pills, potions, and powders can never help us. Then we try to overcome in our own strength by trying to work more, getting rid of stuff we think is weighing us down, and trying to struggle through. That won't work either.

> For we are not fighting against flesh-and-blood enemies, but against evil rulers and authorities of the unseen world, against mighty powers in this dark world, and against evil spirits in the heavenly places. (Ephesians 6:12 NLT)

You will also notice that Jonah wasn't even aware of the storm that was taking place. Sometimes we are the last ones to notice the storm we are causing around us. Take an addict for example. Everyone else will see the storm of the addiction before he or she admits it to himself or herself. It's affecting everyone but the person is still asleep to the fact that he or she is causing some terrible issues. Maybe the person needs to get up and do something different. Maybe the person is like Jonah and decides to run away from the place called there. Maybe he or she is on the boat and being affected by someone like Jonah.

We can usually find ourselves in this reading somewhere or know someone who is. If you're a Jonah, then repentance and turning back to God are needed. If you are on the boat, then you need to wake up that Jonah in your life, tell him or her about the God you serve, and tell him or her that Jesus is the way, the truth, and the life. It wasn't too late for Jonah and it's not too late for you or anyone you know.

DAY 46

Jonah answered, "I am a Hebrew, and I worship the Lord, the God of heaven, who made the sea and the land." The sailors were terrified when they heard this, for he had already told them he was running away from the Lord. "Oh, why did you do it?" they groaned. And since the storm was getting worse all the time, they asked him, "What should we do to you to stop this storm?" "Throw me into the sea," Jonah said, "and it will become calm again. I know that this terrible storm is all my fault." Instead, the sailors rowed even harder to get the ship to the land. But the stormy sea was too violent for them, and they couldn't make it. Then they cried out to the Lord, Jonah's God. "O Lord," they pleaded, "don't make us die for this man's sin. And don't hold us responsible for his death. O Lord, you have sent this storm upon him for your own good reasons." (Jonah 1:9–14 NLT)

Today we continue reading about Jonah's decision to run away from his place called there—a place he didn't want to go. In the above reading, we see Jonah reveal who he was running from. That frightens everyone. They question him on how this violent storm would stop. He tells them, but they still try to get through the storm on their own. They don't want to throw Jonah overboard. They don't really have faith in what Jonah told them. It doesn't seem like it would help, and they probably don't want anything else bad to happen. After struggling long enough, they all realize God is the only true God. They all start to pray to Him.

God always seems to use a bad situation to do something good. The crew on the boat originally believed in other gods that were false, but they saw that the God of heaven was real. They all cried out to Him. Even though Jonah was running away from the call, God was still able to reveal himself to people who didn't know Him yet. That has happened in my life a lot of times. I would have something on my heart. I would run away from that calling, but I would still be used by God to reveal Jesus to others.

Maybe you're on the wrong path now. God can bless the broken road you are on, and others will see His goodness. You can still perform the mission while you are turning around. You might not know a lot, but you know Jesus, and you can tell your testimony. That's really a lot! Don't quit on the call. My friend, I am here to tell you that it isn't too late. God is always good even when we get everything messed up.

DAY 47

Then the sailors picked Jonah up and threw him into the raging sea, and the storm stopped at once! The sailors were awestruck by the Lord's great power, and they offered him a sacrifice and vowed to serve him. Now the Lord had arranged for a great fish to swallow Jonah. And Jonah was inside the fish for three days and three nights. (Jonah 1:15–17 NLT)

The sailors finally listened to Jonah and threw him overboard. The storm ceased and that eased any doubts about God's mighty power. Why do you think Jonah didn't just jump overboard himself? I believe it was fear. He knew that he was the reason for the storm. He knew he needed to get off that boat. I don't know if he trusted that God would show up in the deep waters or not. He needed others to help him get moving.

We see in the New Testament a group of guys carry a guy to church and then rip the roof off the church to get him to Jesus. Everyone is paralyzed by fear from time to time. We must make the decision to follow Jesus for ourselves, but we can't do it by ourselves. Jonah's bad decisions led others to know God, but it also led him into the belly of a fish—a dark and scary place to be in. Then Jonah did something we all should do when we enter a dark place in our lives, like the darkness of depression or that terrible pit of anxiety. He cried out to God. He was in a dark place for three days and nights. Can you think of anyone else who did something similar?

DAY 48

—◆◇◆◇◆◇◆—

Then Jonah prayed to the Lord his God from inside
the fish. He said, "I cried out to the Lord in my
great trouble, and he answered me. I called to you
from the land of the dead, and Lord, you heard me!"
(Jonah 2:1–2 NLT)

Jonah runs in the opposite direction of the place God called him to.
He gets on board with some sailors and sets off with them instead.
His problems cause a big storm for everyone around him, so he
decides that it would be better if he was tossed into the troubled
waters. Now he is in the middle of the storm alone, and probably
treading water to stay alive. At least everyone else is okay and the
storm ceased for them.

Sometimes when you're trying to just breathe and stay alive,
God's provisions show up the most in your life, even if you don't
recognize them as provisions at first. God sends a fish to swallow
Jonah. It is not exactly the best thing in the world, but it saves
Jonah's life. Maybe you are sitting in jail. It is not exactly the best
place to be, but it could be what saves your life. Jonah isn't struggling
physically to stay alive, but he is still in a dark place. I am sure that
he is both physically and emotionally tired. The only thing he could
do was cry out to his God. Tired, alone, and I am sure very scared,
Jonah cries out to God from the pit of his darkness. God heard him
and answered him.

If you do find yourself like Jonah—in a dark place like a jail cell
or the locked ward of a rehab center—you can cry out to God too.
It's not too late for that. Your bad decisions may have put you in this
situation, but God will not leave you. He is always there. Now you
must be willing to admit you are going the wrong direction and cry

out to Him. He will meet you right where you are. His grace will surely overwhelm you. Then it will empower you to get back up and start going in the right direction. When the fish spits Jonah out on dry land, I bet Jonah didn't look like he had it all together. He was probably a mess, but at least he was back where he belonged. God is good!

> Then the Lord ordered the fish to spit Jonah out onto the beach. (Jonah 2:10 NLT)

Read through Jonah's prayer today. It's in chapter two. Read it. Think it. Pray it. Talk about it. Get to know the God who answers you in the pit of darkness.

DAY 49

"Commit everything you do to the Lord. Trust him, and he will help you." Psalms 37:5 NLT

We saw how God had a plan for the life of Elijah, Jeremiah, and Jonah. He has a plan for you too. He has a place called there He wants to take you to. Sometimes we get to know where that place is, and sometimes we don't. Sometimes we get to know what the purpose of going there is, and sometimes we don't. God's ways aren't like our ways. However, the first step of faith is the same for all of us. We must believe in our hearts and confess with our mouths that Jesus is the Lord of our lives. That will start you on a journey. Then if you commit everything you do to God and trust Him through everything, you will see that He is helping you. You will do things that you never thought would be possible and you will see things that you never thought were possible. Commit your life to Him and trust Him through everything that happens. Maybe your place called there is sobriety. Maybe it's called taking that new job. Maybe it's called forgiveness. Whatever the place called there is for you, it's going to be a beautiful place. Your faith and His grace will take you to unimaginable places in your life. Take that first step and go.

DAY 50

Fire tests the purity of silver and gold, but the Lord tests the heart. (Proverbs 17:3 NLT)

It's easy to trust God when everything is going well, and you know exactly how things will turn out. What about right now? In this cell? At this very moment? Do you still trust Him? Do you think you are ready to go back into society and never be back in this situation again? Is your heart ready?

Even the most precious metals are tested for purity. When all the impurities are burned away, the metal is left in its purist form. Gold becomes twenty-four karats after it goes through the fire. How much more important is your heart to God? King David faced a lion and a bear before Goliath. Even Jesus was sent to the wilderness for forty days to be tempted. Those are just a couple of examples. Can you praise Him even when you don't feel like it? Can you still seek Him even if the outcome isn't exactly what you wanted? Can you love your neighbor even when he or she isn't very lovable? Can you serve even when you aren't appreciated? God wants to purify our hearts so love will infiltrate every place we go and so others can see God.

God blesses those whose hearts are pure, for they will see God. (Matthew 5:8 NLT)

Your best days are ahead of you. God is just getting started with you. Today your heart is a little bit purer than it was yesterday. Your heart is at the center of everything you do.

Then Christ will make his home in your hearts as you trust in him. Your roots will grow down into God's love and keep you strong. (Ephesians 3:17 NLT)

DAY 51

❖❖❖❖❖

Elijah was afraid and fled for his life. He went to Beersheba, a town in Judah, and he left his servant there. Then he went on alone into the wilderness, traveling all day. He sat down under a solitary broom tree and prayed that he might die. "I have had enough, Lord," he said. "Take my life, for I am no better than my ancestors who have already died." (1 Kings 19:3–4 NLT)

We previously read about Elijah going to a place called there. He was obedient to God's instruction, and everything was going well for Elijah. He knew God personally and trusted Him. Still the evil of depression hit this mighty man of God when he heard that Jezebel wanted to kill him. He only heard about this, and it opened the door to depression. If you go back and read about Elijah in the previous chapters, you will find out some of the extraordinary things that God did through him. One evil report against him was able to send him running away, much like Jonah did. The information about Jezebel caused the evilness of depression.

If you meditate on an evil report long enough, the fear will send you running away too. That can lead to wanting to be alone and isolating yourself. The depression is invited into your life. Depression can be caused by several different things, but I do know that running away to be alone can make it worse. Maybe you find yourself slipping off into depression. Be honest about it, get some help from others, and turn back to God. Depression isn't a sign of weakness or something to be ashamed of. It's another part of life that you need to do something about. Maybe you need to do something differently. Reach out to others and don't isolate yourself. Get some help if you need to.

That's why I wanted to share my heart with you on this matter. I know all about it and have been through it too. I can tell you that there is hope. There's a God who cares. It isn't too late to turn your life around. If you're sitting in a jail cell thinking this just won't end, that it will be a long time before you get out, that maybe suicide is the way out—don't go that route. That's not God's plan for you. That's the voice of the enemy and not God's. The enemy can't take your life, but he is always trying to get you to take your own or maybe even someone else's.

> "The thief does not come except to steal, and to kill, and to destroy. I have come that they may have life, and that they may have it more abundantly." (John 10:10 NKJV)

However, there's hope in front of you. There are better days ahead. You are here on purpose and for a purpose and the world is better because God has put you in it. No matter what you have done or what was done to you, that purpose is still alive. God is speaking to your heart right now. It's a gentle whisper. He does not always speak in big, dramatic ways of the earth. It is often a whisper: "What are you doing here, (insert your name here)?" Most of the time it's a question for you. I believe that it is to pull stuff out of your heart and so you can confess it. He knows the answer. God is a good, good father!

> "Go out and stand before me on the mountain," the Lord told him. And as Elijah stood there, the Lord passed by, and a mighty windstorm hit the mountain. It was such a terrible blast that the rocks were torn loose, but the Lord was not in the wind. After the wind there was an earthquake, but the

Lord was not in the earthquake. And after the earthquake there was a fire, but the Lord was not in the fire. And after the fire there was the sound of a gentle whisper. When Elijah heard it, he wrapped his face in his cloak and went out and stood at the entrance of the cave. And a voice said, "What are you doing here, Elijah?" (1 Kings 19:11–13 NLT)

I got through it. Once in a while, the enemy will try to bring that heaviness on again but God gets me through it. You're not alone. You don't have to be alone.

Even when I walk through the darkest valley, I will not be afraid, for you are close beside me. Your rod and your staff protect and comfort me. (Psalms 23:4 NLT)

Remember that you're here for a reason. I am praying for you to see yourself the way God sees you.

DAY 52

As he was approaching Damascus on this mission,
a light from heaven suddenly shone down around
him. He fell to the ground and heard a voice saying
to him, "Saul! Saul! Why are you persecuting me?"
(Acts of the Apostles 9:3–4 NLT)

Before God changed his name to Paul, he was known as Saul. Saul
was persecuting the followers of Christ. One day he was on a mission
to do more of that in Damascus, but everything changed for him
on the road that day. Do you remember when everything changed
for you? Maybe you were on a mission too—a mission to get more
alcohol, sell some drugs, have an affair, rob someone, or whatever it
was that day. It was a mission that you had carried out many times
before, but this time God showed up on the road. That day, the light
came on in your life. Maybe it was in the back of a cop car or in
the hospital intensive care unit—whatever knocked you down and
finally got your attention. More than likely it didn't happen like it
did for Saul that day. Maybe your eyes didn't see the light and you
didn't hear the audible voice of Jesus. I believe you could have, but
for me it wasn't exactly like that. I accepted Jesus and was baptized
in 2000. That wasn't the moment the light came on for me. You need
a personal encounter with the Holy Spirit to have that happen. Yes,
my heart was made right, but without the Holy Spirit, I couldn't live
the way God was calling me to.

Saul believed in God and thought what he was doing was a good
thing. He was legalistic and religious until he was on the road to
Damascus. I believed but didn't follow. I went through a divorce,
and I turned to the bottle instead of the Lord. I started on my
Damascus Road and it landed me in the intensive care unit. God

tried getting my attention several times and in many ways before that day. I was always under the influence, which is what the devil uses alcohol to do to us. You can't understand anything when you're under the influence. On May 13, 2007 was the last drink of alcohol I ever had, and I was knocked down. It took another four years for me to have the clarity to understand that God was calling me to him. My light coming on wasn't as quick as Saul's, but for me, personally, it was just as dramatic. On May 13, I was trying to destroy my life forever and I believe God's intervention saved my life. I won't go into all the details, but the doctor told my family he didn't think I would make it. Someone somewhere was praying for me. I believe that.

Maybe you are on the road to Damascus right now. Let these words that I write turn the light on for your life. Maybe you know someone struggling along his or her Damascus Road. Keep praying for that person. Your prayers are making a difference! That supernatural encounter could happen on any given day. Also, I realized that I wasn't walking in love like God wanted me to and that type of life hurts Him. Jesus asked, "Why are you persecuting me?" That question made the light in my life a little brighter.

DAY 53

When the servant of the man of God got up early the next morning and went outside, there were troops, horses, and chariots everywhere. "Oh, sir, what will we do now?" the young man cried to Elisha. "Don't be afraid!" Elisha told him. "For there are more on our side than on theirs!" Then Elisha prayed, "O Lord, open his eyes and let him see!" The Lord opened the young man's eyes, and when he looked up, he saw that the hillside around Elisha was filled with horses and chariots of fire. (2 Kings 6:15–17 NLT)

Maybe after you had your Damascus Road, you had a moment a lot like Elisha's. You accepted Jesus into your life, but you had to deal with the natural consequences of your previous actions. Then one day, you wake up and receive a call from loved ones about the troubles that are surrounding them. The first thing you need to do is pray that their spiritual eyes will be opened, and they will be able to have the clarity to see God in the middle of everything. They might be surrounded by addiction, pain, depression, severe anxiety, financial issues, or medical problems. Pray that the Lord opens their eyes and lets them see that all of their troubles are surrounded by His love and goodness. There is pain and there are problems, but God's grace is there too. Those storms are real, but so is that rainbow. His promises are true no matter what. Once your loved ones see that rainbow, everything will start to be different. They will be looking for the rainbow in every storm instead of listening to thunder that's roaring loudly. With that comes a peace that can only come from God. Don't worry so much about your loved ones that are still on the outside of faith in God. He loves them even more than you do. Pray for them. Speak life in to them. Let them watch you be transformed by God. Then they will see that you are a beautiful rainbow in the storm called life. Let your true colors shine in the darkness. Others need to see that happening. Be that rainbow.

> "I have placed my rainbow in the clouds. It is the sign of my covenant with you and with all the earth." (Genesis 9:13 NLT)

DAY 54

For you bless the godly, O Lord; you surround them
with your shield of love. (Psalms 5:12 NLT)

When you have your spiritual eyes opened, you will start getting to
know that shield of love. You will see that you are surrounded by
His amazing love. That love is always present for you to reach out to.
I believe that is what prayer does. It allows us to connect with His
love from the natural. It's always there, but we need to receive it into
our lives. When you get an early morning call that your daughter
is going to the emergency room because of post-surgery problems,
you pray first. You bring God's love into it. He has it surrounded.
Whenever you get some bad news, I encourage you to pray before
doing anything else.

They do not fear bad news; they confidently trust
the Lord to care for them. (Psalms 112:7 NLT)

Bring God into everything you do. You get some good news, say
a prayer of thanksgiving. Wake up every morning and say, "Good
morning, Lord." Invite Him into your day right away. Having a bad
day with God's love is a lot better than having a great day without
it. Bad never stays bad for very long and great without Him is a
deception. God has you surrounded. Ask Him to reveal that shield
of love to you today.

DAY 55

Every word of God proves true. He is a shield to all who come to him for protection. (Proverbs 30:5 NLT)

The word of God is true, and you can always trust it. God will be a shield that protects you from making those unwise decisions. When you start a journey with God, it's His word that will keep coming up inside of your heart whenever you face those temptations that led you astray before. They will convict you and then redirect you. We all make mistakes and start down the wrong path from time to time. His word is alive and active. It comes up inside of you and will penetrate right through any thoughts you are having. The flesh of course wants to go against the word, but your spirit (heart) is getting stronger! Every day that you spend studying His Word is another strength training session. Being physically fit is good but being spiritually fit is even more important.

Here are some examples of how this has worked in my life. I am working in the jail and someone who is under the influence comes in. The person isn't being nice and is saying ugly stuff to me. That activates the Word inside of my heart. It sounds like this: *God is an ever-present help in my life. He has me surrounded. Love covers a multitude of sin, and this person needs to see that love regardless. That person is under the influence of the devil's substances and doesn't know His love yet. He is with me.*

Another example might be when I see an inmate really struggling emotionally. I can reach out to that person. I get that prompting in my heart. It sounds like this: *Love your neighbor. That's your neighbor struggling. Go pray with them and bring Me into their life. Remember that you were once broken too. Broken crayons can still color beautiful pictures. Be a rainbow in their storm.*

One last example is if I am making a wrong decision or saying something wrong. A gentle anxiety will come upon me—not that evil overwhelming anxiety, but like an alert to pray, and to make a different choice because the decision I'm about to make goes against the Word. Then the check engine light comes on.

> But the Holy Spirit produces this kind of fruit in our lives: love, joy, peace, patience, kindness, goodness, faithfulness, gentleness, and self-control. There is no law against these things! (Galatians 5:22–23 NLT)

Know the word of God helps give me the discernment to make better choices. Anything that doesn't line up with the word isn't God's prompt. That's important to know too. There's a lot of evil out there trying to get your attention.

> For the word of God is alive and powerful. It is sharper than the sharpest two-edged sword, cutting between soul and spirit, between joint and marrow. It exposes our innermost thoughts and desires. (Hebrews 4:12 NLT)

Trust His Word and study it daily. You will never leave a study time the same person. God is good always!

DAY 56

Elisha told him, "Get a bow and some arrows." And the king did as he was told. Elisha told him, "Put your hand on the bow," and Elisha laid his own hands on the king's hands. Then he commanded, "Open that eastern window," and he opened it. Then he said, "Shoot!" So, he shot an arrow. Elisha proclaimed, "This is the Lord's arrow, an arrow of victory over Aram, for you will completely conquer the Arameans at Aphek." (2 Kings 13:15–17 NLT)

Maybe you are still dealing with the enemy that is also known as the flesh. That's the part of you that will always be in rebellion to the things of God. It's not born again like your spirit or renewed like your soul. It needs to be crucified daily. That can be a fight of faith sometimes. In the Old Testament, God spoke through His prophets. Today, God speaks through His Word and the Holy Spirit to each one of us personally.

"My sheep listen to my voice; I know them, and they follow me." (John 10:27 NLT)

King Jehoash of Israel was struggling with an enemy by the name of the Arameans. I compare that enemy to our flesh. We need deliverance from that enemy that is always rebellious. We need to follow the word of God and by the power of the Holy Spirit, we can completely conquer that enemy. Elisha gave the king a word. Faith is an action. King Jehoash got some arrows and a bow. Then notice the next thing that happened. Elisha put his hands on the king's hands to help him shoot the arrow of the Lord. If you put everything in God's hands, you will see God's hands in everything. The Holy Spirit will not only help give you the strength to shoot but also the direction to shoot in. Open the Eastern window! The Lord's arrow of victory will go ahead of you, and you will be victorious.

Maybe that addiction is still a struggle for you. Get a word from God and apply it to your life. Do that every single day. You will get the victory. You go one day without using. Victory! You resist one temptation today. Victory! Celebrate each victory because there's no such thing as a small victory when it comes to God's way of living. The cross is your arrow of victory. You can do all things through Christ. Jesus has made the way. Your spirit and soul are now strong enough to overcome everything the flesh desires. I believe in you. More importantly is the fact that God believes in you.

> For I can do everything through Christ, who gives
> me strength. (Philippians 4:13 NLT)

DAY 57

Then he said, "Now pick up the other arrows and strike them against the ground." So, the king picked them up and struck the ground three times. But the man of God was angry with him. "You should have struck the ground five or six times!" he exclaimed. "Then you would have beaten Aram until it was entirely destroyed. Now you will be victorious only three times." (2 Kings 13:18–19 NLT)

Never give up on praying for a situation or a loved one. Today, we look at the rest of the story with Elisha and the king. Elisha told him to pick up the other arrows and strike them on the ground. The king only struck the ground three times. We need to keep on striking the ground until we destroy the enemy. Repeat after me: keep on praying, keep on praying, keep on praying. Remind yourself to keep on praying. You're tired. Keep on praying. You don't see the enemy destroyed. Keep on praying. You don't see your loved one serving God. Keep on praying. Don't give up on your prayers. They are working behind the scenes. You don't see a tree when it's first planted in the ground, but it's growing. The work is taking place behind the scenes. Keep on praying!

DAY 58

The next morning as they were leaving Bethany, Jesus was hungry. He noticed a fig tree in full leaf a little way off, so he went over to see if he could find any figs. But there were only leaves because it was too early in the season for fruit. Then Jesus said to the tree, "May no one ever eat your fruit again!" And the disciples heard him say it. (Mark 11:12–14 NLT)

The next morning as they passed by the fig tree he had cursed, the disciples noticed it had withered from the roots up. Peter remembered what Jesus had said to the tree on the previous day and exclaimed, "Look, Rabbi! The fig tree you cursed has withered and died!" Then Jesus said to the disciples, "Have faith in God." (Mark 11:20–22 NLT)

Let's continue to talk about what happens behind the scenes in the spiritual realm. Jesus gives us a great example of this, and He also shows us the power of our words. Jesus noticed that something in His grace wasn't producing what it was supposed to be. He cursed it by speaking to it. It wasn't needed in His life. Anything that isn't producing the fruit you need, you have the authority to curse that thing right out of your life. Your words are faith containers that you release into the spiritual realm. There are some things that you pray for, but there are some things you must pray against. You speak with the authority you have by using the name of Jesus.

This fig tree wasn't producing anything to feed him, so it was out of order and useless. There was no need to have that in His life. When He spoke to it, the word went to work on that tree immediately, even though no one noticed any changes at first. It went to work at the roots, which is an example of the spiritual realm, the unseen part of life. Later, on the way back, Peter noticed that it withered up at the roots and died. He seemed surprised by this, and Jesus told him to have faith in God.

Maybe you have been dealing with an out of order fig tree in your life. Your body isn't doing what it's supposed to do, or maybe it's that spirit of anxiety causing you issues. Whatever it is, use your words by faith to curse that junk. Talk to that sickness or evil spirit. Curse them in Jesus's name. Maybe your loved one isn't serving God yet. Speak life-filled words in Jesus's name. The words will go to work for you even before you see it. Don't stop believing or praying just because you haven't seen it yet. Have faith in God. God is good even when life isn't.

DAY 59

Then the Lord said to Moses, "Lift your hand toward heaven, and the land of Egypt will be covered with a darkness so thick you can feel it." So Moses lifted his hand to the sky, and a deep darkness covered the entire land of Egypt for three days. During all that time the people could not see each other, and no one moved. But there was light as usual where the people of Israel lived. (Exodus 10:21–23 NLT)

The darkness was so thick that they could feel it. It had everyone paralyzed. They couldn't see anything, and I am sure the feeling of that darkness was an overwhelming sense of constant anxiety. Darkness is the absence of light. The Israelites had light the whole time that darkness was plaguing Egypt. It wasn't about what was happening around them, but Who was with them. Even when the world around you is in darkness, you can still live in light. Every born-again believer has that light dwelling within him or her.

One thing the COVID virus did was reveal who really had the light. They started to shine brighter and brighter the darker the world became. COVID paralyzed most of the world, including most of the churches. Fear spread faster than the virus and caused more problems than the actual virus did. Eventually a lot of people started to notice the light some carried within them: people going to work without fear, people not afraid to lay hands on sick people, people talking about faith not the fear. One scripture that I stand on is this: "Do not dread the disease that stalks in darkness, nor the disaster that strikes at midday" (Psalms 91:6 NLT).

The virus is stalking around in the darkness. You can't see it, but everyone seems to be feeling it. I say if God said it, then I believe it. I don't have to live in the dread of the darkness. I can keep on being the light and you can too. This devotional was being conceived during this time and now is birthed to help shine some of that light. Maybe you are currently dealing with the darkness of depression or addiction. That's darkness that you can physically feel. I know a little about that. It can paralyze you and keep you isolated. You are tired, and your body hurts; this darkness even inflicts pain on the other people you love, and your health often declines. It costs you a lot more than just money, but money problems can manifest too. Everything starts falling apart in your dark life.

I am here to tell you to take one step towards the light. Worship for fifteen minutes today, read the word for fifteen minutes today, pray for fifteen minutes today, and give to someone or even serve somewhere. All these things will help you turn the lights on. Don't stay in that darkness. Take one step through it. It's a valley you can keep walking through. The devil is a liar! Don't quit moving by faith. God is with you. How do I know? You are reading this and that means you are seeking Him. That type of hunger comes from the Holy Spirit. Keep on walking! David did, and you have something better than God with you. You have Him within you!

> Even when I walk through the darkest valley, I will not be afraid, for you are close beside me. Your rod and your staff protect and comfort me. (Psalms 23:4 NLT)

> The life of the godly is full of light and joy, but the light of the wicked will be snuffed out. (Proverbs 13:9 NLT)

> For once you were full of darkness, but now you have light from the Lord. So live as people of light! (Ephesians 5:8 NLT)

DAY 60

$\diamond\diamond\diamond\diamond\diamond$

For God has not given us a spirit of fear, but of power and of love and of a sound mind. (2 Timothy 1:7 NKJV

Today let's talk about how the enemy will use fear to control you. Let me give you a personal example of how this happened to me and how you might be able to relate to this in your life too. Let me help you bring some scriptures alive in your heart and be an overcomer of this type of fear. It happened suddenly and out of nowhere. I had this sense of fear whenever I had to travel out of town anywhere. I don't really know exactly why this happened to me, but it wasn't good. It made me feel physically sick to my stomach every time I had to go anywhere. It didn't matter where I was going either. I hated it, and it kept me home most of the time. Once I got to where I was going, that feeling of heaviness would leave and then on the ride home, I would be just fine. This experience was telling me that this was going to be a spiritual fight. Every time that I surrendered to the fear and stayed home, the next time I went to leave, the fear would be even more intense. When I would go by faith, I would end experiencing a sense of peace that only comes from God. Peace is my favorite thing that God blesses us with. It is better than anything else! One way I was able to break through this fear was to put on my headphones and listen to Chris Tomlin's music. I was able to fix my focus on God and that peace would overwhelm me. I also recited this scripture when that fear come on me.

> Be anxious for nothing, but in everything by prayer and supplication, with thanksgiving, let your requests be made known to God; and the peace

of God, which surpasses all understanding, will guard your hearts and minds through Christ Jesus. (Philippians 4:6–7 NKJV)

I knew that fear wasn't something God wanted for me, but it was something He wanted me to break through by faith. I often had to take anxiety medications before leaving because it was getting bad. You let the devil in the back seat of your car, and he will want to drive. He was trying to drive and steer me in the wrong direction. By the grace of God, I have overcome this problem but there are days when the enemy tries to put that spirit of fear back on me. It's something I will probably have to fight the rest of life because the enemy always tries the same tactics. I wanted you to know that you can overcome the fears that the enemy is trying to direct your life with. What I can do, you can do too. Partner with God and you can do anything. Meditate on His Word and not the fear. Worship your way through it. The peace of God will consume you and you will know how awesome it is to break through your fears! Fear is a liar, and the devil is a terrible driver. You are going to be okay. Trust Him through it all.

DAY 61

"But listen carefully to everything I command you today. Then I will go ahead of you and drive out the Amorites, Canaanites, Hittites, Perizzites, Hivites, and Jebusites. Be very careful never to make a treaty with the people who live in the land where you are going. If you do, you will follow their evil ways and be trapped." (Exodus 34:11–12 NLT)

Instead, clothe yourself with the presence of the Lord Jesus Christ. And don't let yourself think about ways to indulge your evil desires. (Romans 13:14 NLT)

It's easy to listen to the Word of God but it can be hard for some of us to apply it to our own lives. God will go ahead of you. He said that He would. He will drive out all those enemies for you, but you must apply what you heard in order to live in that promise. The devil will be sending all sorts of enemies at you, like fear, anxiety, addiction, depression, confusion, and sickness. It would be easy to make a treaty with any of those because your flesh wants to be comfortable and take the easy way out. It's easy to go along with that addiction because your body won't rebel against it. As soon as you decide to try breaking free from that addiction, your body starts to get a little anxious. That starts by just thinking about trying to break free. Trusting God to help you seems impossible at first. The devil is a liar and a deceiver. What he offers is false hope, fake peace, and lust, not love. The enemy goes to work on the five natural senses: seeing, hearing, tasting, smelling, and feeling are what the liar works on. God gives us what I call a sixth sense to live by; that's called faith.

> For we live by faith, not by sight. (2 Corinthians 5:7 NIV)

It can be easy to make a treaty with the enemy. That bottle of booze looks good. It sounds good too. It will dull my senses to this world. It tastes good, so I had better have another one. I am feeling good now! This is awesome! My life doesn't even stink anymore! The stench was actually coming from the enemy. Faith gives you discernment to see past the physical. That bottle of booze looks good, but I see what will happen to my life if I even take one drink. It sure sounds good. It promises no pain, but pain should push us to God more often. It's letting you know there's a problem that needs addressed. I remember that drink tasted good too. Then I remembered the bitter taste it left in my mouth the next morning. I even smelled bad—that combination of stale beer and sickness. The good feeling was completely gone. Not only was the pain of the world back, so was the pain of a hangover.

Now that I am sober again, I remember the Word of God I had heard before about this. Now the enemy will go to work on the physical senses again but with condemnation. He isn't good but God is! Just because I am writing this devotional doesn't make me immune to the struggles. They are real and preset in my life too. I have overcome a lot, but I still have a lot more to overcome. Without the power of the Holy Spirit in my life, the enemy would completely destroy me. We need God's presence to live the abundant life He wants for us. If you tried before and failed, that's okay. What isn't okay is making a treaty with the enemy, and then just living that way for the rest of your life because it's easier.

> One of the men lying there had been sick for thirty-eight years. When Jesus saw him and knew he had been ill for a long time, he asked him, "Would you like to get well?" (John 5:5–6 NLT)

God is asking you the same question today. The word *well* here actually means whole. Do you want to be whole? Do you want to be spiritually and physically healed, and set free from the devil's treaty and bondage? Stand up, pick up your mat (what's holding you down) and start walking by faith.

> Jesus told him, "Stand up, pick up your mat, and walk!" (John 5:8 NLT)

Be made whole! In Jesus's Name! Amen! You will be set free from what's holding you down. I believe that.

DAY 62

So whether you eat or drink, or whatever you do, do
it all for the glory of God. (1 Corinthians 10:31 NLT)

This is a scripture that I would like to have rooted deep inside of my grandson's heart. I also want to leave it for you to meditate on so that it can take root deep inside of your heart too. Maybe you are asking yourself, *Why this scripture?* I am glad that you are asking that question, because in a world full of choices and influences, you need to have something inside your heart that helps give you discernment, the ability to make good decisions and let positive influences into your life. This scripture coming up in your heart during those moments will help you out. For instance, if my grandson is offered some drugs by "friends" who are telling him how awesome they are, he can decide if this will give glory to God or not. Hopefully he will think, *Grandpa keeps telling me that I need to do everything in ways that bring God glory. Even what I put into my body matters.* Hopefully he will make the right decision more often. I know I need this word too. It isn't just for you and my grandson. I need this in my heart too! We all do. God whispers this question to us with everything that we face. Does this bring glory to God? I feel the conviction of the Holy Spirit even as I type that out. Powerful word to have rooted inside of your heart.

Maybe you are like me and have that special person that you want to influence for God. Sow the seeds of faith into his or her heart with this scripture. Then pray for God to send people who will help water those seeds. The world doesn't appear to be getting any easier to navigate, but that shouldn't be the main influence in your life. Jesus should be. Read about how He lived, and strive each day to be more like Him. There are times that I struggle with this, and there are times where I can hardly believe how far I have come.

CONCLUSION

Jesus replied, "I tell you the truth, unless you are born again, you cannot see the Kingdom of God." (John 3:3 NLT)

The title of this devotional might have you asking why 62 days? Whenever God has me do anything, it's not usually normal. Like God having Noah build an ark before anyone even knew what rain was. It didn't make any sense. I wanted to just do thirty days and not even publish it. That wasn't right. 30 days, 60 days, or even 365 days would seem like good numbers, but God put 62 days on my heart. One reason is just to get your mind to have a sense of wonder before you even open the book. The title gets the mind going a little bit on the question of why; then the heart gets ready to seek the information. The other reason is that six plus two is eight. I Googled the biblical meaning of eight in the Bible. The number eight represents a new beginning. A new beginning is what we all need. Everyone needs to be born again. My hope and prayer is that the words contained in this book inspire you to seek God and find that new beginning. If it helps at least one person, then it's a success.

Spending 62 days in the word will change a person. Every time you study the word of God, it brings new revelation. Now take a moment to remember what you were like 62 days ago and compare it to how you are now. Write down everything that comes up in your heart. I hope you are a little different, or at least have started a relationship with God. Thanks for giving 62 days in the Word your time and devotion.

If you haven't taken the first step yet and accepted Jesus into you, here is a little prayer that you can say to help you get started with God:

> Jesus, I have lived for too long without you in my life. I know that I am a sinner and that I cannot save myself. No longer will I close the door when I hear you knocking on the door of my heart. I am ready to trust you as my Lord and Savior. I believe that You are the son of God and that You died upon the cross for my sins. Then on the third day you rose up out of the grave and set me free. I believe that your words are true. Come into my heart now and make me into a new person. Thank you for saving me and loving me. I will now live my life in the name of Jesus. Amen!

> This means that anyone who belongs to Christ has become a new person. The old life is gone; a new life has begun! (2 Corinthians 5:17 NLT)

If you just received Jesus as your Lord and Savior, let me be the first person to say congratulations on making the best decision of your life! Welcome to the family of God! Remember, salvation isn't just a prayer—it's a new way of life. Stay close to God and always keep the faith. Even when the life around you isn't good, God is still good! May God bless you the rest of your days.

BIBLIOGRAPHY

Carroll, Lewis. *Alice's Adventures in Wonderland*. Project Gutenberg. Last modified October 12, 2020. https://www.gutenberg.org/files/11/11-h/11-h.htm

Ripp, Andrew. "Roses." *Evergreen*. Andrew Ripp Music, 2021.

Printed in the United States
by Baker & Taylor Publisher Services